Daughters of Abraham

Florida A&M University, Tallahassee
Florida Atlantic University, Boca Raton
Florida Gulf Coast University, Ft. Myers
Florida International University, Miami
Florida State University, Tallahassee
University of Central Florida, Orlando
University of Florida, Gainesville
University of North Florida, Jacksonville
University of South Florida, Tampa
University of West Florida, Pensacola

Daughters of Abraham

Feminist Thought in
Judaism, Christianity, and Islam

EDITED BY YVONNE YAZBECK HADDAD
AND JOHN L. ESPOSITO

UNIVERSITY PRESS OF FLORIDA

GAINESVILLE · TALLAHASSEE · TAMPA · BOCA RATON
PENSACOLA · ORLANDO · MIAMI · JACKSONVILLE · FT. MYERS

First cloth printing, 2001
First paperback printing, 2002

08 07 06 05 04 03 02 C 7 6 5 4 3 2
08 07 06 05 04 03 02 P 6 5 4 3 2 1

Library of Congress Cataloging-in-Publication Data
Daughters of Abraham: feminist thought in Judaism, Christianity, and Islam /
edited by Yvonne Yazbeck Haddad and John L. Esposito
p. cm.
Includes bibliographical references (p.) and index.
ISBN 0-8130-2103-0 (cloth: alk. paper)
ISBN 0-8130-2594-X (paperback: alk. paper)
1. Women in Judaism. 2. Feminism—Religious aspects—Judaism. 3. Women in
Christianity. 4. Feminism—Religious aspects—Christianity. 5. Women in Islam.
6. Feminism—Religious aspects—Islam. I. Haddad, Yvonne Yazbeck, 1935–.
II. Esposito, John L.
BM729.W6 D38 2000
291.1'783442—dc21 00-053662

The University Press of Florida is the scholarly publishing agency for the State
University System of Florida, comprising Florida A&M University, Florida Atlantic
University, Florida Gulf Coast University, Florida International University, Florida
State University, University of Central Florida, University of Florida, University of
North Florida, University of South Florida, and University of West Florida.

University Press of Florida
15 Northwest 15th Street
Gainesville, FL 32611–2079
http://www.upf.com

Contents

Foreword

human being

1st Chapters in the Bible OT

The three Abrahamic religions are all adamantly opposed to the subjection of one human being by another. All three insist that men and women were created in God's image and that both sexes have equal rights and responsibilities before God. All cherish the memory of strong, resourceful women who played a key role in salvation history. And yet, in common with most of the major world faiths, none of which has been unreservedly good for women, each of the three has pushed women into an inferior and marginal position, excluding them from full participation in the social, cultural, and religious life of the community. Even though such seminal figures as Jesus, Saint Paul, or the Prophet Muhammad had a positive view of women, relied on them, and treated them as valued colleagues, some of the most revered sages, theologians, and jurists have preached outright misogyny. In recent years, women of all three traditions have challenged this patriarchal hegemony.

workforce

Some have argued for a radical revision to correct the prevailing chauvinism, which, they claim, regards women not only as outsiders but as less than human. Women have made great strides. They have been ordained as rabbis, ministers, and priests. They have written theological and legal works to contest a hitherto unchallenged male supremacy. But this religious feminism has inspired great hostility, including sometimes from other women, who, for example, have been some of the most vociferous opponents of the ordination of women to the Christian priesthood. This volume, which includes the proceedings of a conference held at the Center for Muslim-Christian Understanding at Georgetown University, is an attempt to look at this perennial problem once again. The religious oppression of women has been one of the great flaws of mono-

theism. Despite the fact that it militates against fundamental principles
of their faith, Jewish, Christian, and Muslim men have all hijacked the
revelation and made it conform to the old, unredeemed patriarchy.

The Jewish Bible is a thoroughly realistic text. The book of Genesis,
for example, is quite clear that relations between the sexes are problematic and fraught with suffering. It tells the story of a holy family that is
dysfunctional, and in which husbands and wives are often at war. Yet
even though Genesis is undoubtedly a patriarchal text, it does not provide Jews or Christians with a blueprint for the oppression of women.
The very first chapter insists that man and woman were both created in
God's image.[1] In the garden of Eden, Eve may have been the first to
disobey, but she is a far more adventurous and attractive figure than
Adam, who comes across rather as a stooge, lagging behind his wife and
feebly passing the buck when things go wrong. When Abraham treats
his wife Sarah exploitatively, putting her into Pharaoh's harem to save
his own skin, this provokes a destructive chain of events in his own
family, as we shall see later. In the next generation, it is the vigorous
Rebecca, not the blind, paralyzed, and ineffectual Isaac, to whom God
speaks and who takes control of the family fortunes. And Jacob's cruelty to his wife, Leah, has appalling consequences, leading to murderous
sibling rivalry among his twelve sons, and the text tacitly but strongly
condemns his callous indifference to the rape of his daughter Dinah
(Leah's offspring) by the men of Shechem.

In later books, the Bible treasures the memory of women who became
the saviors and guides of their people: Deborah, Judith, and Esther. And
yet in these pages we see that women were pushed—literally—to an ever
more remote corner of the synagogue, were identified with the Evil Impulse, excluded from the *minyan*, the prayer quorum, and their voices
were not heard. Men would claim that calling women to the *bimah* to read
the Torah would result in the destruction of Judaism. In Jewish law, women
are marginal creatures, excluded from mainstream social and religious
life, like children and slaves. As one Jewish feminist observed, woman
was "The Jew Who Wasn't There."

There is a similar paradox in Christianity. Jesus had women disciples
who traveled with him and helped to support him financially. When he
visited his friends Martha and Mary at Bethany, he praised Mary, who
preferred to sit at his feet, like any male rabbinical student at the feet of
his master, rather than help Martha in the kitchen. When Jesus was ar-
rested, it was, in the main, only women who had the courage to stay with
him throughout the crucifixion, while the male disciples went into hid-
ing; and, according to the gospels, it was women who had the first news

of the resurrection. Saint Paul insisted that in Christ there was neither male nor female; the old gender inequality, like the inequalities of class and race, was gone for good.[2] He spoke of women as his co-workers in ministry.[3] On only one occasion, when he commands the women of Corinth to wear their veils when they prophesy in the assembly, does Paul allow the chauvinism of his time to get the better of him.[4] Most of the passages attributed to Paul that relegate woman to a subordinate position—in the epistles to Timothy, for example,[5] were written long after Paul's death by a Christian who wrote in his name to indicate that he was Paul's disciple. Saint Luke is the evangelist who is closest in spirit to Paul, and of the four gospels his is the most positive toward women.

So Christianity was originally good news for women, but at an early date the gospel was made to serve patriarchal chauvinism. Like their Jewish counterparts, Christian women were also marginalized and pushed away from their menfolk. Saint Augustine told his priests to leave women strictly alone; if they were sick or in trouble, another woman could tend them. "What does it matter whether we speak of a wife or a mother?" he wrote to a friend. "It is still Eve, the temptress, of whom we must beware in all women." Saint Augustine made the doctrine of original sin central to the Western Christian vision; and since it was Eve who was the first to pluck the forbidden fruit, women, sex, and sin became fused in the Christian imagination. For in Christianity, besides bearing the usual burden of a perceived inferiority, women were also castigated for their sexuality. More than any other major faith, Christianity has found it difficult to integrate sexuality with the sacred. Several of the fathers of the Church, particularly in the West, equated marriage with prostitution. They saw sexual love as inherently sinful and incompatible with a true Christian life. Saint Augustine saw his conversion to Christ as inseparable from a vocation to chastity. The only good woman, in the Christian view, was a virgin: by denying her sexuality, a woman became an honorary man.[6] Whereas in Judaism and Islam, women received honor and a measure of respect from being wives and mothers, for the greater part of Christian history, celibacy was the top vocation. It was not until the seventeenth century that Christian matrimony became truly holy.[7]

Christian women often had to bear the brunt of men's disgust with their own sexuality. Luther's sexual attitudes, for example, were thoroughly Augustinian. He believed that sex was inherently sinful, but that marriage covered it with a veneer of respectability so that "God winks at it."[8] Despite his own marriage, Luther had little time for women, who were to be punished for Eve's sin by exclusion from public life. A woman, he decreed, was to remain in the home "like a nail driven into the wall."[9]

Like Christianity, Islam began with a very positive message for women. Indeed, the faith can be said to have come to birth in the arms of a loving woman. When Muhammad received the first revelations of the Qur'an, their impact was so shattering that he used to crawl, trembling convulsively, to his wife Khadija, who cradled him in her lap until his fear subsided. Muhammad was one of those rare men who actually enjoyed and sought out the company of women. Women were among the first converts to Islam, and the Qur'an gave women rights of inheritance and divorce that Western women would not receive until the nineteenth century. As Amira El-Azhary Sonbol points out in her chapter, although there is some debate about the position of Arabian women in the pre-Islamic period, it seems clear that women played an active role in the early Islamic community in Medina. The Qur'an prescribes neither the veiling of all women nor their seclusion in the house of their male protectors; but some three or four generations after the Prophet's death, Muslims imitated the customs of the Greeks and the Persians in their new empire, who had long treated their women in this way. Muslims also picked up some of the Christian misogyny. Like all pre-modern legal codes, the *shari'ah* reduced women to the rank of second-class citizens, even though the ideal of the equality of all believers was crucial to the Qur'an's message. Sonbol points out that jurists habitually interpreted Qur'anic injunctions with a patriarchal bias that proved damaging to women.

The improved status of women was one of the most significant developments of the twentieth century. It has irrevocably changed the social, domestic, intellectual, and economic life of society. But, sadly, religious people, who should be in the forefront of this process of emancipation, have often tried to put women back in their old marginal place. In all three of the Abrahamic religions, the more conservative believers have responded to the emancipation of women in modern culture by overstressing traditional restrictions. Haredi Jews have been known to attack members of their ultra-orthodox community who allow their wives and daughters to infringe the strict dress code.[10] In Haredi districts, placards implore the Daughters of Israel to dress modestly. In some Muslim circles, the veiled woman has become a sign of the integrity of Islam; and in the United States, Protestant fundamentalists—men and women alike—see feminism as one of the great evils of our time. Husbands feel unmanned and obscurely castrated by the spectacle of the empowered woman.[11]

In all three faiths, the embattled religiosity known as "fundamentalism" fears annihilation at the hands of the secular and the liberal establishment, and it seems to be the case that when a community feels imperiled, women's bodies become the focus of concern and attention. In the fifth century C.E., when the barbarian tribes (some of whom had converted to heretical forms of Christianity) were bringing down the Roman empire in Europe, Saint Ambrose of Milan used to make celibates stand like boundary stones around the altar when Mass was being said, to protect its sanctity. At the same time he made the virginal body of Mary, the mother of Jesus, a symbol of true Christianity, which must remain forever unpenetrated by the errors of the invading barbarians.[12] In this volume, Leila Gal Berner shows how the Talmudic rabbis responded to the loss of Jerusalem and the temple in 70 C.E. by a stricter interpretation of the segregation of the sexes in the synagogues, to hold the Evil Inclination in check. Today, when fundamentalists fear the destruction of true faith, the bodies of women have once again become the focus of acute anxiety. They must be shrouded, protected, and secluded from the inimical world, like the endangered community itself, which often withdraws from mainstream society to create an enclave of pure faith and builds new barriers against an invasive secularism.

But, fears apart, the marginalization and oppression of half the human race is sinful, and it impairs the integrity of all three of the monotheistic religions. This book is valuable because it shows Jewish, Christian, and Muslim women cooperating together to correct the abuses of the past. This does not often happen. Women in all three traditions have usually colluded with the prejudices of their menfolk, and have even condoned the persecution, deprivation, and denigration of people who belong to a different faith. It is a sad fact of human nature that suffering does not always make us better people. In the biblical story of Sarah and Hagar, explored in these pages by Amy-Jill Levine, we see women who have been damaged by patriarchy abusing one another.[13] Sarah, whom Abraham treated as chattel when he put her into Pharaoh's harem, later treats her Egyptian slave Hagar (whom she may unconsciously associate with this humiliation) with similar contempt. When she gives Hagar to her husband, so that Abraham might finally conceive a son, she never mentions her by name. Hagar has ceased to be a person to her. When Hagar becomes pregnant, she seems to taunt Sarah. In this male-dominated household there is enmity between the two oppressed women, which finally results in Sarah's forcing Abraham to send Hagar and Ishmael out into the wilderness to face almost certain death.

But the story also illustrates that even though Isaac is, according to the Bible, the son of the promise for Israel, Hagar and Ishmael are also chosen. In the wilderness, Hagar receives a divine revelation on a par with that vouchsafed to the Jewish patriarchs. She too "sees God";[14] her son will also be the father of a great nation, and he will become a prophet of Islam.

Everybody is chosen, even if his or her election belongs to another story. One of the challenges that women must face as they become more empowered is not to fall into the old chauvinisms regarding other faiths, traditionally seen as rivals, pretenders, heretics, or infidels. Instead of using their experience of oppression to subjugate others, like Abraham's two wives, they should use their suffering to empathize with the oppression of others. Instead of simply getting even and becoming the equals of men, women will then have brought something new and positive to the religious scene and transformed faith for the better.

Yet before they can make any such contribution, women have to be taken seriously as the religious equals and even the leaders of their menfolk. Here, Hibba Abugideiri's fine essay on Hagar as a model for "gender jihad" contains valuable insights. She points out that, even though Hagar is not mentioned explicitly in the Qur'an, she provides a model of Islamic leadership and reform. Hagar reminds us that faith is not characterized by passivity but demands that women as well as men take the initiative. Her female activism—when, despite her faith that God would provide for her and Isma'il in the desolate region of Mecca, she ran tirelessly between the mountains of Safa and Marwah to find water for her son—has been recognized by all Muslims as exemplary. In the *hajj* ritual of *sha'a'ir*, it has become one of the pillars of Islamic consciousness. Hagar is buried with Isma'il beside the Ka'bah, at the heart of the Islamic world. For centuries, in all three monotheistic faiths, however, women have been marginalized and pushed to the periphery of religious life, even though this violates crucial monotheistic teachings. Men as well as women must now engage in a jihad, a struggle to make explicit and normative what has been tacitly acknowledged: that women must be admitted to the precincts of sacred orthodoxy on a par with men, and, if their insights and faith warrant it, should become their leaders, as Hagar led and guided the Prophet Isma'il.

Karen Armstrong
Leo Baeck College for the Study of Judaism

Notes

1. Genesis 1:27.

2. Galatians 3:27–28.

3. Romans 16:1–16.

4. 1 Corinthians 11:2–12. The demand that "women are to remain quiet at meetings" (1 Corinthians 14:34) is generally held by scholars to be a later addition to the epistle and not contributed by Paul. It interrupts the sense, contradicts Paul's earlier assumption that women *will* speak and prophesy in meetings, and is uncharacteristic of his style.

5. 1 Timothy 2:9–15.

6. Karen Armstrong, *The Gospel According to Woman* (London: Anchor, 1986), 1–87, 117–69.

7. Ibid., 259–77.

8. Lectures on Genesis 3:16, in *Patrologia Latina*, ed. J. Minge, 50 vols. (Paris: n.p., 1864–84), 34:395–96.

9. Letter to Wolfgang Ressenbusch, as quoted in *Sex in Christianity and Psychoanalysis* by W. G. Cole (London: Dent, 1956), 114.

10. Ehud Sprinzak, "Three Models of Religious Violence: The Case of Jewish Fundamentalism in Israel," in *Fundamentalisms and the State*, ed. Martin E. Marty and R. Scott Appleby (Chicago and London: University of Chicago Press, 1993), 465.

11. Michael Lienesch, *Redeeming America: Piety and Politics in the New Christian Right* (Chapel Hill: University of North Carolina Press, 1993), 52–76.

12. Peter Brown, *The Body and Society: Men, Women, and Sexual Renunciation in Early Christianity* (London: Columbia University Press, 1988), 352–56.

13. Genesis 16, 21:1–21.

14. Genesis 16:7–14.

Introduction

Women, Religion, and Empowerment

℧℧

JOHN L. ESPOSITO

Int chapters of O.T.

The three great Abrahamic traditions (Judaism, Christianity, and Islam) have much in common. Despite significant differences, their religious worldviews reflect a shared heritage: belief in one God, prophets, and revelation, values that emphasize ethical responsibility and accountability. Similarly, all three have struggled with the challenges of modern life and produced diverse responses, from conservative to reformist.

Although, as Karen Armstrong notes in her Foreword, Jesus, Saint Paul, and Muhammad had positive views of women, later theologians and scholars of sacred law imposed a patriarchal hegemony that at times degenerated into androcentrism and misogyny. Thus, a key issue in religious reformation or reconstruction has been gender relations, in particular the status of women. However different, the daughters of Abraham, Sarah, and Hagar have inherited a religious legacy that is not only the product of divine revelation but also of human interpretation, the Word of God mediated through the words of human beings, overwhelmingly male and patriarchal. The primary interpreters of sacred texts have been males functioning in and thus reflecting the attitudes and values of male-dominated societies. Sacred texts have been interpreted in specific contexts. Differences in interpretation reflect both the reasoning of individual minds as well as diverse cultural contexts and local customs. As a result, the image of women has been shaped by patriarchy as much as by revelation.

meaning ?

As theological and legal interpretations have endured down through the ages, the line between sacred revelation or law and human interpretation has often become blurred or forgotten. Thus, human-generated contextual responses have often been transformed and equated with unchanging, divinely revealed or mandated dogmas and laws. Patriarchal theologies, interpretations, symbols, structures, and institutions have too often become sacralized and entrenched.

Beginning in the late 1960s and 1970s, all three faiths witnessed significant attempts to address issues of gender. Among the many catalysts were modernist and reformist movements within the traditions as well as feminist and liberation movements. This process has required and generated not only reassessments of the role of women in the past but also studies that attempt to reinterpret and reconstruct. In all three faiths women's organizations and movements have critiqued the legacy of patriarchy, which is the silence or absence of women in religion, and they have called for widespread reforms that emphasize a more egalitarian, inclusive, nonsexist approach. Women have demanded their rightful places in the synagogue, church, and mosque. Increasing numbers with theological training have claimed their role as interpreters of their religious tradition. As Amy-Jill Levine observes, "Feminist interpreters of scripture and tradition, having recognized that the objects of their studies can serve both oppressive and liberationist purposes, do not all espouse the same reaction." While some reject the traditions and the texts that support them, others choose to reclaim, rewrite, or re-edit them or to create new traditions. In the "Structures and Strictures" section of her chapter, Levine discusses the multiple roles of Sarah and Hagar in the Bible, their relationships to Abraham and to each other. Presented and interpreted as a polarity, Sarah in Genesis and in Saint Paul's Epistle to the Galatians symbolizes that which is desirable, promised, and legitimate while Hagar is alien and rejected. However, more recent Western interpretations introduce new insights into the text as interpreters "find their own voice in the encounter with the text." They reverse the more traditional interpretations and instead see Sarah (and Abraham) as the oppressor and Hagar as the oppressed. As Phyllis Trible observes, Hagar becomes "the faithful maid exploited, the black woman used by the male and abused by the female of the ruling class . . . the resident alien . . . the other woman . . . the expelled wife . . . the divorced mother with child . . . the welfare mother."[1] This reinterpretation flows from a process of emphatic reclamation by which feminists reread traditionally marginalized figures. Levine endorses this method for its ability to provide a new appreciation of both self and other. However, she warns that interpreters must avoid the pitfall of setting up a new polarity and thus simply reversing the roles of Sarah and Hagar as oppressor and oppressed rather than appreciating the complexity of their roles and functions. Moreover, they must also be willing to critique biblical characters as, for example, they would American Caucasian Christian men: "The boundary between critical assessment and empathy is a narrow one, hedged with parochialism (e.g., blaming the victim) on the one side and paternalism (e.g., idealizing the victim) on the other."

Just as the stories of Sarah and Hagar are incomplete and remain open to allegorical interpretation and to emphatic reclamation, they are open to new meanings. Though their scriptural characters remain separated, their daughters and sons do come together in tradition. Thus, Amy-Jill Levine concludes: "Respecting each other's cultures and beliefs while celebrating their own, responsive to each other's needs while responsible to their own community's concerns, Christians, Muslims, and Jews, daughters of Sarah and Hagar, may yet bring peace to the family of Abraham."

The "absence" or marginalization of women has often been most visible in worship. Though in the first and early second Temple in Jerusalem, men and women worshipped together, gender segregation in ritual celebration became the norm by the Talmudic period and the voices of women came to be disregarded by male shapers of Jewish liturgy. While some feminists choose to study and reinterpret texts, others believe it necessary to create new space for women within their respective religious traditions, for women, as Levine observed, whose "heartfelt voices raised in song and celebration have generally been ignored by male shapers of Jewish tradition."

In contrast to those who are content to carve out a place for women within the ritual realm of Judaism and traditional Jewish law (*halakha*), Leila Gal Berner represents those contemporary Jewish women who create new paths, new rituals that embody and express the experiences of women. In her chapter, "Hearing Hannah's Voice: The Jewish Feminist Challenge and Ritual Innovation," Berner revisits and rereads the experience of Hannah, the first Jewish woman in Hebrew scripture to raise her voice in prayer, an act the Jewish tradition recognizes as the first example of "personal prayer." The text is emblematic of the ritual differences between men who emphasize structure and ritual "rules" and women who stress a more personal and emotional relationship. So today, after centuries of exclusion or marginalization, Jewish women en-

I've always had "trouble" w/ ritual!

gage in ritual innovation to incorporate and give expression to the "uniquely female experience of the Divine," the particular ways in which women approach spirituality and prayer.

Inspired by the secular feminist movement, Jewish women in the 1970s pressed for inclusion as equals in Jewish institutions and ritual life, pressing on such issues as rabbinical ordination and access to leadership positions in synagogues and national Jewish organizations. They sought to alter the status and function of women in Jewish religious law (halakha), striving to reconcile feminist claims with Jewish law. However, Berner believes that despite the gains, the progress made reflected a "band-aid approach" that "did not address the more deeply systemic feminist challenge of 'liberation,' rather than simple inclusion." In contrast to their predecessors, members of the second generation of Jewish feminists wish to "bake a new pie" that goes to the core of Judaism. Rather than attempt to accommodate themselves to a male-designed structure, feminists seek to reshape the structure to meet their needs as well as those of men. The goal is to liberate women from a framework in which the normative is male and they are defined as other, and to develop a more integrated model that embraces women's full humanity. Hannah responds to the High Priest Eli, who found her personal prayer so incomprehensible that he attributed it to intoxication: "I have my *own* way of speaking to God . . . I *am* free to pray in this way!" So too, Berner maintains, Jewish feminists today proclaim, "We have our *own* way of engaging with Judaism. And in approaching Judaism in our own way, we bring about our own liberation. The Jewish 'pie' must be baked anew to combine the ingredients of a millennia-old tradition with a deep, contemporary feminist consciousness." Thus, "normative" will be redefined to give equal value to female and male perceptions of reality and experiences of religious and spiritual life.

Just as in Christianity and Islam, reformers address the "silence" or absence of women through historical research that seeks to recover the "lost voices" of women in past centuries who served as leaders and who contributed to the development of religion and spirituality. They engage in scriptural studies and a new exegesis that often asks new questions and often finds fresh answers: "What pain must Hagar have felt at her banishment into the desert with her son Ishmael? Did Sarah really want Hagar's death? . . . Why was Miriam punished for demanding her rightful place of leadership alongside her younger brother, Moses?" Of equal importance, Jewish feminists fill the silence by writing a "new" Torah text with their own lives. Drawing from their experiences as women, Jews, and human beings, they provide a new narrative to in-

~~form and shape an evolving Jewish tradition. Berner, who has herself been involved in creating new Jewish rituals with a feminist perspective, discusses the development of a healing ritual for survivors of sexual abuse. She places it within the broader desideratum that Judaism's evolving tradition should include within its liturgical repertoire the life experiences of contemporary women and men.

Although several women were ordained in the late nineteenth century, it was well into the latter half of the twentieth century when women's ordination became more widely accepted in Christian denominations. Women were excluded from ordination because they were not theologically prepared, having been denied a theological education. As Alice Laffey notes in her chapter, "The Influence of Feminism on Christianity," winning access to theological education, which led many women to recognize the extent to which patriarchy permeated scripture and tradition, initiated a process of deconstruction and reconstruction. If some like Mary Daly, an early critic of patriarchy's domination of traditional theology, left the Church, other feminists have chosen a "more moderate course." Mastering church history, scripture, theology, and spirituality, they identify and critique the patriarchal character or paradigm of scripture and tradition in order to develop a liberating theology through a process of reinterpretation and reconstruction. Laffey describes and assesses the impact of several prominent feminist scholars in theology as well as Old and New Testament studies. She then provides two of her own examples of a rereading (deconstruction and reconstruction) of scripture that finds new meanings in two Old Testament texts. The first is a feminist biblical reading of the book of Esther, in particular as it regards Vashti. Employing what she describes as "a perspective of liberation, a hermeneutics of suspicion, and a hermeneutics of imagination," Laffey illustrates how a "decentered interpreter can provide a biblical reading that shifts power relations." A similar rereading of Numbers 22 enables Laffey to demonstrate the results of an eco-feminist reading of the encounter between an ass and the prophet Balaam. Though an animal, the ass speaks and behaves in a way that is more laudable than the human beings she encounters. While she is personal and relational, and appeals to interdependence, Balaam's ignorant and violent actions are conditioned by his patriarchal values of power and hierarchy.

Alice Laffey's eco-feminist reading of this text, like her feminist reading of Vashti in Esther, produces new insights and values that redress patriarchal and hierarchical biases and interpretations. They underscore the extent to which Christian feminists work "toward a future in which power can be shared, hierarchical relationships can be replaced by relationships of reciprocity and mutuality grounded in a profound respect for human and cosmic interdependence."

In only thirty years, Christian feminist theology has become global in scope, extending from North America, Latin America, and Europe to Asia, Africa, and the Middle East. Despite the fact that it was not until the 1960s that women became an accepted presence in theological education, feminist theologians have proven prolific, producing a rich corpus of literature, scholarly in origin but practical and pastoral in scope. In Chapter 4, "Christian Feminist Theology: History and Future," Rosemary Radford Ruether, a leading voice, summarizes the purpose of feminist theology: "we need to do feminist theology as a corrective to a theology distorted by patriarchy, in order to create a holistic or inclusive theology, a theology that . . . would liberate women and men from sexist ideology and practice."

Influenced by the patriarchal cultures and social context of the Hebrew and Greco-Roman worlds and their medieval and modern descendants, Christianity long excluded women from its official teachings on theology, spirituality, and sexuality, as did Judaism and Islam. Where women were visible, their contributions were often constrained by a patriarchal church. Echoing her Jewish scholar-predecessors in this volume, Ruether speaks of the historical absence or silence of women, their inability to "enter into conversation about God and humans, good and evil, truth and falsehood, sin and salvation, from their own vantage point." The male elite experience was considered normative. Thus, Christian theology taught the ontological necessity of God's being male and that men were God's redemptive ministers, leaders of the church and interpreters of scripture and tradition. Women were either seen as the source of evil, irrational or immoral, or idealized as mothers but unfit by their nature to teach and minister. God was imaged in male terms, in terms of power and hierarchical relationships, while women were the corresponding objects of subjugation and domination, exploitation, and injustice.

Ruether provides a perspective on feminist theology's global quest for an alternative tradition in scripture and history, the attempt by theologians to reclaim and reconstruct the symbols of faith and move from androcentric misogyny to an egalitarian, liberating inclusiveness and mutuality. Broader common theological symbols and doctrines such as God language, Christology, church, ministry, sin, and salvation are reclaimed and reconstructed. Using these conceptual tools, a theology of liberation addresses shared concerns of gender oppression and subjuga-

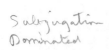

tion, exploitation, and violence against women, the poor, and the earth. In the developing nations, many of which still struggle from the effects of their religious colonization by Christianity, local issues are pressing. Among the more prominent are socioeconomic and cultural colonialism, neo-dependency, and exploitation. However, despite the rapid growth of feminist theology and its accomplishments, Ruether underscores the theological and socioeconomic struggles that persist in a world in which male dominance and androcentrism still prevail.

Increasingly in recent years, we have come to realize that talk of a Judeo-Christian tradition encompasses only a partial historical and theological reality. The global presence of Islam, the second largest of the world's religions in numbers of adherents—and, in particular, its presence today as the second- or third-largest religion in America and Europe—has brought a growing recognition of a Judeo-Christian-Islamic tradition. As the children of Abraham, Sarah, and Hagar share much in common theologically, so too Muslim women, the daughters of Hagar, share much with the daughters of Sarah. In increasing numbers, they are also engaged in a reexamination and rereading of scripture, tradition, and history, and a reinterpretation and reconstruction of the present.

In Islam, Hagar does not carry the same exegetical significance that she does in Judaism and Christianity. While her role and mission are significant, Hagar has not enjoyed the same visibility in Islamic texts and discourse as Sarah (and even Hagar) in Judaism and Christianity. Hibba Abugideiri, in "Hagar: A Historical Model for 'Gender Jihad,'" argues that this absence is not due to her sex but rather to the lack of any dispute regarding her significance. As Hagar was the mother or ancestor of Abraham's heirs, the Muslims, with a sacred mission so too today, Abugideiri maintains, she constitutes "an exemplary and powerful figure for demonstrating how female struggle [jihad] and liberation remain integral aspects of Muslim women's modern lives, only now they are imbued with different meaning in response to contemporary issues."

Despite the relative paucity of texts and information about Hagar's life, Hibba Abugideiri shows how, though born a slave, she is chosen to be a messenger of God and the matriarch of Muslims, and is a powerful exemplar for contemporary female reformers. Despite distinctive differences, parallels can be drawn between her life and that of the Virgin Mary, the only woman mentioned by name in the Qur'an and interestingly named more often in the Qur'an than in the New Testament. Hagar is the recipient of a revelation from God delivered by an angel

Messina

who informs her of her divine mission, the name of her son, Isma'il, and Isma'il's future as a prophet with his own mission. Hagar's deep-seated faith or God consciousness (*taqwa*) and her actions become a source of Muslim belief and ritual and a model for female reformers today. The example of her faith in God and her frantic search, running seven times between Safa and Marwah looking for water in the desert for her son, are commemorated by those who perform the hajj or pilgrimage to Mecca each year. At the same time, the example of her God consciousness (taqwa) and courage combined with self-initiative and activism, are the qualities that Abugideiri believes are an enduring legacy to women today.

Leadership in Islam may be found in many forms; not all roles are gender specific. Thus, women from the Prophet's wives to the scholars and sufis (mystics) have exercised leadership. Yet, patriarchy prevailed historically as men became the primary political, religious, and intellectual leaders, while women were often marginalized in the mosque and public spaces. The only major area where women's leadership role has been acknowledged is in regard to issues that are perceived to be specific to women. However, even that role has been circumscribed by the power and control of men, the *ulama* or religious scholars, as guardians of religion, formulators and interpreters of law, and judges.

Hibba Abugideiri demonstrates how three Muslim female reformers embody the qualities of Hagar in responding to contemporary contexts. They use the authority of sacred scripture to argue for gender equality: "a reconfiguration of the traditional Islamic paradigm, not because [gender jihad] pits the category of woman against that of man, but . . . [because it] seeks greater complementarity between the sexes, as based on the Qur'an." However different, they share a God centeredness (taqwa) and challenge the notion of Islamic leadership as a male-dominated prerogative, thus changing the way both leadership in Islam and Islam in general are understood.

The Qur'an and Islamic law are central to defining and redefining the status and role of Muslim women. Amina Wadud and Amira Sonbol (a contributor to this volume) have played significant roles as scholars and voices for reform nationally and internationally. Wadud's hermeneutics in *Qur'an and Woman : Rereading the Sacred Text from a Woman's Perspective* provides a new approach to reading the Qur'an from a more gender-inclusive perspective. Her deconstruction and then reconstruction of Qur'anic concepts and passages challenges the exclusion of females as formative voices of Qur'anic scholarship and the resultant tendency that privileged patriarchy and the male experience as normative. Wadud's analysis emphasizes the Qur'anic message of gender equality and inclusiveness, the role of women as agent and not just subject. Distinguishing between text and context, the universal and the particular, the eternally valid and culturally specific, Wadud argues for a methodology that enables reinterpretation and reform.

Sonbol, through her own ground-breaking writings and those of other scholars with whom she collaborates, has challenged the common assumption that Islamic law is inimical to women and that modern secular reforms have necessarily been liberating. She has not simply focused on texts but on contexts, on how Islamic laws have been interpreted and applied in diverse historical circumstances. Thus, Abugideiri notes, Sonbol demonstrates that "Muslim women of different Muslim countries were historically better positioned and had more contributing power to personal status laws . . . when the law was based on the more flexible and evolving legal system of Islamic jurisprudence, rather than the rigidity of codified secular law."

Finally, Sharifa Alkhateeb offers an example of contemporary female activism. In a world in which men have dominated American Muslim organizations, she has provided a prominent model of female leadership in the Muslim community. Alkhateeb created and served as president of the National American Council for Muslim Women (NACMW). The Council has emphasized education and activism, encouraging women's involvement in public life. It has addressed a range of major issues, from violence against women and low-interest loans for economic ventures to health care and female genital mutilation. Alkhateeb and NACMW have assured a major Muslim women's presence in international forums such as the United Nations Fourth World Conference on Women in Beijing, and she served as a consultant to the White House.

As Hibba Abugideiri concludes, the contribution of these Muslim reformers, however different, is multidimensional. They provide unique models of leadership in that they liberate women from long-standing misogynist biases, carve out a female presence not only in public space but within Islamic orthodoxy, and thus, in reforming women's issues, reform Islam itself.

If there has been one image that has symbolized Islam and Muslim societies in the popular mind, it is that of veiled, secluded women and with it their subjugation. As Abugideiri notes: "The normative view of Muslim women presents them as victims of a patriarchal order defined by Islamic laws, traditions, and norms." For many scholars, social activists, feminists, and the media alike, the inequality of women in Islam is an unquestioned fact. Ironically, both Western critics and many Muslim apologists identify and characterize the fundamental sources for gender status and relations as the Qur'an and Islamic law. The static, medieval nature of law and of women's legal status was reinforced by the so-called closing of the door of *ijtihad*, the belief that after the tenth century jurists could no longer interpret or reinterpret Islamic laws. Modern legal reforms, especially those in personal-status law (laws governing marriage, divorce, and inheritance), were depicted as countering the patriarchy of the past. In her chapter, "Rethinking Women and Islam," Amira El-Azhary Sonbol challenges these and other misconceptions.

Using Ottoman and Egyptian archival records, Amira Sonbol demonstrates that historically Islamic law was dynamic rather than static. The application of law in the courts was influenced by differences of time and place and by differences of opinion among jurists. Moreover, many Muslim women were active rather than simply subjugated and passive in the courts: "Women appeared in court routinely. . . . buying, selling, marrying, divorcing, reporting violence, demanding compensation, custody of their children." Failure to distinguish between textual sources and the legal opinions of scholars and judges in actual historical and social contexts has obscured and distorted the dynamism of the past, replacing it with a vision of an unchanging body of law interpreted by medieval religious scholars. Sonbol, while recognizing the accomplishments of nation states in improving the status of women, challenges the conventional wisdom that modern legal reforms countered the patriarchy of the past and necessarily improved the rights of women: "in practice women experienced a marked deterioration in gender relations under what can only be called state patriarchy since the state extended its authority over all matters of family, gender, and personal relations." The flexibility of the Islamic courts was now replaced by a fixed system of new laws selectively and superficially based on Islamic law that often limited rather than liberated.

Like Amina Wadud, Amira Sonbol argues for a more dynamic and inclusive understanding of the Qur'an. She maintains that conservative clerics today as in the past engage in a selective, nonhistorical, misogynist reading of the Qur'an and Islamic history that perpetuates patriarchal hegemony and a moral hierarchy. Sonbol engages in a rereading of critical Qur'anic passages and Islamic history often used to support gender inequality and argues from textual analysis and historical criticism that the Qur'an supports gender equality in family relations, marriage, and divorce.

At the dawn of the twenty-first century, women in the Abrahamic traditions continue to reconstruct their faith traditions. As this volume demonstrates, all engage in rereading scriptural texts and history to counter the patriarchy and male-centered norms of the past and present. They seek to empower themselves and to reconstruct the symbols, doctrines, laws, and institutions of their religious traditions, replacing patriarchal hegemony with a more inclusive and egalitarian religious vision. Reform has occurred in differing contexts; the extent and pace of change has varied from one tradition to another. However, as the following chapters indicate, the daughters of Abraham, Sarah, and Hagar are, in their own distinctive ways, rediscovering and reclaiming, addressing the silence and absence of women in the past, and taking their rightful place as equal partners in determining the future of Judaism, Christianity, and Islam.

Notes

1. Phyllis Trible, *Texts of Terror: Literary-Feminist Readings of Biblical Narratives* (Philadelphia: Fortress Press), 28.

Societal
Religions   > when two
              combine   "bad" for 9s

Philosophic religions become regions

Line in the Sand / Dirt

1

Settling at Beer-lahai-roi

꩜

Amy-Jill Levine

Structures and Strictures

In October 1994, Professors Alice Laffey, Amina Wadud-Muhsin, and I participated in the first of a two-part series; our task was to address the topics of religion and feminism as they relate to Muslim/Christian understanding and as they are placed in the contexts of scripture and tradition. In March 1995, three other panelists would address the same topics and the same focus, but they would do so under the rubrics of issues and prospects. Thus we have a series of pairs: Sarah and Hagar; Muslim and Christian; religion and feminism; scripture and tradition; issues and prospects; even meetings in October and March, in 1994 and 1995. We were, moreover, sponsored by two groups: Georgetown University's Center for Muslim-Christian Understanding (itself a coupled designation) and the Department of Theology.

I emphasize the pairs first because feminist theory teaches awareness of the dangers of dualism: pairs usually presuppose or impose distinctions that render one element of the couple superior to the other. Which of the two takes precedence—Sarah/Hagar, black/white, man/woman, Jew/Gentile, Sunni/Shi'ite, Catholic/Protestant, Orthodox/Reform— is arbitrary but nonetheless weighted. The point is not that one member of the pair is intrinsically better; it is that we (ourselves, our discourses, our cultures) assign privilege. Moreover, these hierarchies can become polarized and then reified; in such cases, one element is idealized while its opposite is condemned. The phenomenon even occurs with pairs that are not usually identified as opposites. For example, "religion," defined parochially, is not infrequently contrasted to "feminism," defined in a similarly narrow manner. Which of the two, religion or feminism, is vilified depends upon the person or group assigning the definitions.

These arbitrary oppositions are called into question by the arrangements of the panels: three, rather than two, were invited to speak on each occasion. And there I was, a Jew who studies early Christianity, asked to speak for a Center of Christian-Muslim Understanding.[1] Dualisms can be interrupted by the introduction of a new category or a new mode of investigation, as long as that third category is not appropriated by one element of the pairs or otherwise forced to take sides.

The various configurations of the panel participants—according to religious confession, textual expertise, ethnic background, and so forth —served as well to complicate allegiances and perspectives. Feminist theory shares with postmodernism the observation that we all have conflicted and often conflicting loyalties; we all speak from or assume or occupy various "subject positions." Muslims disagree with Muslims, Jews with Jews, Christians with Christians. Women—as the Genesis accounts of Sarah and Hagar painfully demonstrate—do not always act in solidarity. In feminist and interfaith dialogues, loyalties shift: at times I find myself allied with women from different religious traditions; at times my perspective matches that of other Jews, both men and women. I variously define myself primarily as woman, Jew, mother, Caucasian, American, feminist, heterosexual, and liberal. Nor is this list exhaustive. In turn, these and other labels will be either implicitly or explicitly assigned to me by the Georgetown audience and by readers of this essay. The attendant connotations of such labels are for some neutral or positive; for others, they are demonic. In my view, "feminist" conveys a positive force for bringing shalom, in the fullest sense of peace and wholeness; to others it represents a fundamental—and essentially negative —threat to social good, moral responsibility, and "family values" (and the same points hold for words like "Muslim" or "Jew" or "Christian").

Because we engage in multiple, interested, conflicted, and over-determined readings, we all bring to texts and traditions under investigation certain agendas, many of which are tacit and already embedded in the discourses and methods we employ. Nor does the text sit in isolation; it too brings along its history of interpretation.[2] Our language immediately demonstrates the situated nature of inquiry. When I speak of "scripture," I refer to the Tanakh;[3] my colleagues may refer to the "Old and New Testaments" or to the Qur'an. My "tradition," dependent on that scripture, includes midrashic interpretations; my colleagues on the other hand might look to patristic sources or hadith. Reading(s) of Sarah (with an "h" from the transliteration of the Hebrew) and Hagar, from *Bereshit* interpreted through rabbinic lenses, will necessarily differ from those who count Paul's Epistle to the Galatians canonical, or those who see themselves as heirs of Ishmael rather than of Isaac. There is, however, a difference between the acknowledgment of one's own priorities and the marginalization or dismissal of those of others.

In most interpretations of "scripture" and "tradition," professional or canonical pronouncements tend to privilege certain topics and groups and to relegate others to the margins or to ignore them entirely. Material about women frequently appears in appendices to historical and theological works (an appendix, by definition, is a useless, vestigial, but occasionally dangerous, organ); gender and class are rarely adduced as categories of analysis, and heterosexism has only recently become a topic for consideration. The princes of Court and Church are considered more worthy of attention than the peasant and the poor, and views from the European West provide the touchstone by which expressions of colonized peoples are evaluated. These prevailing models define the "conventional wisdom"; they are "the way things have always been done." Consequently, the dominant system inevitably controls the conversation. Even worse, its adherents usually adopt the guise of objectivism, such that their pronouncements appear to be natural or divinely mandated (rather than contingent and culturally constructed.)

Recognition that there are different "truths"—that what is proclaimed helpful or correct by one community may be seen by another equally well-intended and well-informed group as harmful and illegitimate—contributed to the emergence of feminist analysis. Women's lack of access to boardroom and *bimah*, politics and pulpit, economic and medical parity, to the canons of history and literature, then became paradigmatic for the analysis of other power differentials.[4] Feminist analysis accordingly extends to questions of religion, class, race, ethnicity, and sexual preference, among others, and it often remarks on the interrelated or systemic nature of oppressive behaviors.[5] In so doing, feminist analysis necessarily challenges and so threatens the status quo. More, it challenges and so threatens those invested in preserving it.

Feminist interpreters of scripture and tradition, having recognized that the objects of their studies can serve both oppressive and liberationist purposes, do not all espouse the same reaction. Some feminists choose to reject the traditions and the texts with which they were raised and often to which they were once committed. Others seek some form of ongoing relationship by advocating reclamation or reinterpretation of older material and by creating new traditions.[6] Still others remove themselves from any confessional interests and search historical records for accounts of the lives of and cultural reactions to those outside circles of power. The reaction depends on both the text or phenomenon under investigation and the experiences, beliefs, and audiences of the interpreter.[7] These observations hold true in general for matters of scripture and tradition, and they find specific manifestation in the exemplary topic of the present forum: Sarah and Hagar.

The Power and Perniciousness of Interpretation

As with most dualisms, the placements various readers have assigned to Sarah and Hagar are both easily supported and easily reversed. On one hand are interpretations, based on the plot of Genesis and the allegory in Galatians that derives from it, that define Sarah as emblematic of what is desirable, promised, and legitimate and that view Hagar as alien, atavistic, and rejected. On the other are readings that celebrate Hagar as representative of the oppressed: she struggles against elite privilege and social abuse while Sarah epitomizes domination and violence. In each case, typological impulses and empathic reclamations combine to encourage group identification with one character, which can be empowering, and group rejection of the other, which can be harmful.

Key

Paul's Epistle to the Galatians 4:22–26 provides an excellent example of allegorical representation privileging Sarah:

∂ 2 words

> For it is written that Abraham had two sons, one by a slave woman and the other by a free woman. But the one by the slave woman was born according to the flesh, and the other, the child of the free woman, was born through the promise. Now this is an allegory: these women are two covenants. One woman, from Mount Sinai, bearing children for slavery, is Hagar. And Hagar is *Islam* Mount Sinai in Arabia, and this corresponds to the present Jerusalem, for she is in slavery with her children. But the other woman is the Jerusalem above; she is free, and she is our mother. *Christianity*

Sr

A similar typological privileging of Sarah over Hagar, and of Isaac over Ishmael, can be found in *Genesis Rabbah* 47 (to Gen. 17:15–27):[8]

Sr

"religion"
Stories about the writing

A. Said R. Isaac, "It is written, 'All these are the twelve tribes of Israel' (Gen. 49:28). These were the descendants of the mistress [Sarah].

B. "But did Ishmael not establish twelve?

C. "The reference to those twelve is to princes, in line with the following verse: 'As princes and wind' (Prov. 25:14). [But the word for *prince* also stands for the word *vapor,* and hence the glory of the sons of Ishmael would be transient (Freedman, p. 402, n. 2).]

D. "But as to these tribes [descended from Isaac], they are in line with this verse: 'Sworn are the tribes of the word, selah' (Hab. 3:9). [Freedman, p. 402, n. 3: the word for *tribe* and for *staff* or *rod,* in the cited verse, are synonyms . . . so these tribes would endure like rods that are planted.]"

Western interpretations providing a positive reception of Hagar are more recent and usually depend more on metonymic connections rather than on allegorical correspondence. For example, Phyllis Trible introduces her chapter on Hagar with the epitaph, "She was wounded for our transgressions; she was bruised for our iniquities"[9] and thereby evokes both Isaiah's suffering servant and Jesus of Nazareth. Trible also recollects images of Hagar as "the faithful maid exploited, the black woman used by the male and abused by the female of the ruling class . . . the resident alien . . . the other woman, the runaway youth, the religious figure fleeing affliction, the pregnant young woman alone, the expelled wife, the divorced mother with child, the shopping bag lady . . . the homeless woman . . . the welfare mother, and the self-effacing female whose own identity shrinks in service to others."[10] More recently, Delores Williams has raised up Hagar's "slavery, poverty, ethnicity, sexual and economic exploitation, surrogacy, rape, domestic violence, homelessness, motherhood, single-parenting and radical encounters with God" in asking if Hagar's "pain and God's response to it [were] congruent with African-American women's predicament and their understanding of God's response to black women's suffering."[11]

Such readings introduce new insights into the original story (in this case, Genesis); they also allow interpreters to find their own voice in the encounter with the text. For the Galatian Church, Paul provides an entry into the family of Israel; the allegory transforms Gentile-Christians into heirs of the covenant. If the position of Christians advocating circumcision and so conformity to all of Torah is dominant in Galatia, as much of

Godspell

the epistle suggests, then Paul's allegory justifies and encourages those who follow his "gospel of freedom." The rabbis view themselves as the heirs of Isaac; Ishmael, who stands for oppressive Christian Rome, claims the divine blessing but will eventually lose it.[12] Trible reclaims the role of Hagar for the Christian community by giving value to her suffering: her body is metaphorically connected to the broken body of the Christ on the cross. And Williams locates a "Hagar-centered tradition of African-American biblical appropriation."[13]

a Shtetl

Yet, as Elizabeth Castelli astutely argues, "The process of allegory as translation is distinguished by both violence and foreclosure."[14] While all interpretation forces readers to choose narrative elements to highlight and therefore elements to dismiss, allegory intensifies the selection process. Characters become ineluctably translated into abstract categories. In Galatians, Hagar will always be associated with slavery (even though in Genesis she becomes free); Sarah will always be associated with the non-earthly (Jerusalem above, "according to the spirit") and therefore removed from her flesh-and-blood roles as harem pawn, slave-owning wife, and laughing mother. These static associations have, moreover, a life beyond Galatians. The Pauline allegory that first served to legitimate the Gentile Christian apart from the mitzvoth becomes a means of delegitimating those who adhere to Mosaic practices: Sarah becomes the (Gentile) Church freed from the Law while claiming sole interpretive rights to it; Hagar is the (Jewish) Synagogue bound to a literalist and ineffectual exegesis.[15] In readings less nuanced than those of Trible and Williams, not only does Hagar positively become the archetypal minority victim who eventually secures her own future, but Sarah comes to epitomize white, colonialist, patriarchal, and usually "Jewish" privilege.[16]

?

Paul's allegorical interpretation necessarily leads to polarization. In the service of his gospel, he paraphrases the Sarah of Genesis: "What does the scripture say? 'Drive out the slave and her child, for the child of the slave will not share the inheritance with the child of the free woman'" (Gal. 4:30). Similarly, there are today separatists—Israelis and Palestinians, Protestants and Catholics, Muslims and Orthodox—who demonize those they classify as "other," who replace dialogue with dismissal or death. Thus the allegory continues, but it variously highlights divisions of religion, race, ethnicity, class, sexual orientation, and so forth. And it variously produces liberating, and imprisoning, results.

More sensitive to original or at least earlier literary and historical contexts than allegory are empathic feminist reconsiderations of traditionally marginalized or ignored figures. For example, Hagar's wilderness experience has become a paradigm for liberationist concerns: the heavenly message is accorded to one outside the "chosen people"; the slave's affliction is recognized; she receives the promise of offspring that "cannot be counted for multitude"; and she in turn assumes the power of naming Beer-lahai-roi in testimony to her encounter (see Gen. 16:7–14).[17] Sharon Pace Jeansonne correctly notes that "Hagar demonstrates her strength and independence by selecting a wife for her son from among her own people" (Gen. 21:21).[18] An empathic approach to Hagar and the feminist concern to recover the role of the marginalized or victimized combine to encourage the raising of these textually observant and hermeneutically uplifting points.

Empathic reclamation is therefore a reading strategy to be endorsed, and it can lead to new appreciation of both self and other. Problems occur, however, in the facilitation of the empathic process, particularly when it is generated from a position of privilege. Negative resonances that accompany the character in question are not infrequently ignored or excused. In some cases, the previously marginalized, the "other," becomes regarded as invariably right and good. The self, the non-marginal (who is often, ironically, a Western woman and thus herself marginal in still-male-dominated academia), is then wrong and guilty. Moreover, since the "other" is seen as the locus of the good and the desirable, empathic readings from above risk co-opting the identity of and traditions associated with that "other."

When the voice of the "other" (the woman, the poor, the foreigner, the previously silenced) does speak, new benefits as well as new problems arise. These voices add to the multidimensional and multicultural chorus of interpretation; an empathic reception delights when these voices sing their own song in their own key. Yet, as with all performances in the public domain, some are better than others. The negative side of the empathic approach comes when scholars hesitate to apply the same critique to such authors, and such biblical characters, that they would to, say, American, Caucasian, Christian men, lest they seem to be culturally insensitive, racist, xenophobic, or narrow minded. The boundary between critical assessment and empathy is a narrow one, hedged with parochialism (for example, blaming the victim) on one side and paternalism (idealizing the victim) on the other.

Thus, while Hagar's various activities can be celebrated and her various persecutors condemned, it is unhelpful to view her solely as victim or unequivocally as "good." For example, Jeansonne's focus on Hagar correctly yields an image of maternal strength. But had she focused on Ishmael, the same comparative method might emphasize Hagar's infantilizing of her son—for example, her carrying the now teen-aged boy on her shoulder, her choosing his wife (versus the self-choice of Esau and Jacob). Hagar is a complex character: not simply victim and not simply heroine. The same diversity of interpretation, of course, holds for Sarah. Events that suggest strength and self-determination may emerge as much more ambiguous when placed in different narrative contexts, when examined through different methodological approaches, and when interpreted through the lenses of different personal experiences and interpretive communities.

A second example, and a more difficult one, occurs when the positive reevaluation of one figure signals the denigration of another. In such cases the denigration is often neither intended by the author nor recognized by many outside the particular social location of either the figure or the interpreter. Phyllis Trible observes that our knowledge of Hagar "has survived in bits and pieces only, from the oppressor's perspective at that."[19] Trible has herself offered a compelling feminist reading that recuperates Hagar and precisely locates her within a system (literary as well as social) of abuse. Yet still within feminist perspectives, the dialogue can be pressed. Who precisely are these "oppressors": Hebrews? Israelites? Jews? The authors of the text? Men? Are they real people? Undefined, the term "oppressor" is open to various, and potentially harmful, denotations. For some readers, the "obvious" answer—anachronistic and overgeneralized—is "the Jews."[20] For others, the answer is "the text," but this response removes any sense of responsibility even as it erases any rejoinder for those who remain within the canonical traditions.[21] And for everyone, this response expunges speculation concerning the motivations of both author and text: might the story of Hagar have functioned as self-critique or warning? While determining authorial intent and audience impact—or even the "implied author" and "implied audience"—is a necessarily speculative exercise, these very categories can serve to interrupt such assignment of blame.

Once the empathic conversation moves beyond questions of blame, guilt, and the attendant celebration of victimization, fruitful results may be obtained. From the perspective of privilege, the recognition of responsibility can lead to salutary changes; the awareness of readings situated within alternative cultural, religious, ethnic, and class-based perspectives can create a corrective to one's own culturally determined presuppositions. Thus even as readers are multidimensional and are each diversely situated, so too are Sarah and Hagar complex characters enmeshed within their own literary and historical contexts, and ours. The feminist enterprise is then to bring into ongoing, always open dialogue—through rigorous philological investigation, careful historical reconstruction, sensitive literary observations, and awareness of one's own presuppositions—modern readers and the ancient texts.

Scripture and Tradition

Sarah faces an uncommunicative deity, an uninterested husband,[22] consignment to foreign harems, and sterility. Hagar is a slave, impregnated at the will of her mistress and in the bed of the clan leader, sentenced by heaven to return to the house of bondage, and exiled. Sarah procures an heir for her husband, assumes control of Abraham's sexuality, recognizes her decreasing status and seeks to preserve her position, and guarantees her son's inheritance. Hagar flees from abuse, receives a message from heaven, accepts the divine command to return, supports her son, claims the power of naming, and insures her own line. Each woman bears a son—of all the Genesis women, only Sarah and Hagar bear a single child—but each must surrender that child's fate to divine will, for both Ishmael and Isaac face death in the wilderness. Neither has control over her own body, and neither has the support of her natal family. Both are resourceful; both are blessed. Neither is a purely positive role model; neither is a purely negative exemplar.

Genesis 11:29–30 introduces Sarah as follows: "Abram and Nahor took wives; the name of Abram's wife was Sarai, and the name of Nahor's wife was Milcah. She was the daughter of Haran the father of Milcah and Iscah. Now Sarai was barren; she had no child." The matriarch's only independent identification is that she is "barren"; nothing is said of her parents or land of origin.[23] Nothing is mentioned of Hagar's parents, and whereas her ethnicity is known, she appears first outside of Egypt and in the service of Sarah. Thus, like the mistress, the slave is displaced.

Genesis Rabbah poses that Hagar is the daughter of Pharaoh,[24] in which case she mirrors Sarah in the Pharaoh's harem: both are elite foreign women placed by others in sexual service to the dominant man of the nation. Both are also the catalysts for fears expressed by those who ostensibly control them. Just as Abraham is built up materially by Sarah's sexuality, so Sarah hopes to profit by Hagar's fertility "that I may be built up through her" (Gen. 16:2).[25] Abraham and then Pharaoh feel threatened by Sarah's presence in Egypt; Sarah in turn feels threatened by Hagar and Ishmael.[26]

Rather than depict the women as isolated characters, the biblical text intertwines their two stories: the concerns of the mistress bring about the reactions of the slave, and the reactions of the slave inform the characterization of the mistress. Athalya Brenner observes that "paradigmatic pairs [like Sarah and Hagar] are bound tightly together in many ways, so much so that no single member of a given pair is a full personality in her own right but just a psychological segment. The two women complement each other: viewed together, as parts of one single entity, they might constitute a satisfactory image of one person."[27] Yet, perhaps such connections serve to complicate and enrich the already-complete image of each. Just as Sarah is first a component of Abraham's description (one might think of "Mr. and Mrs. Abraham") but then achieves self-determination, so Hagar begins as Sarah's property but will not remain so.

The unity to which Brenner refers is partially masked by the staging of Genesis, since Sarah and Hagar never speak face to face. Instead, exchanges take place over the bodies of their husband and their sons. The conversation begins when Sarah states directly to Abram, "You see that the Lord has prevented me from bearing children; go in to my maidservant; it may be that I shall obtain children by her" (Gen. 16:2). Her rhetoric is political and manipulative: she indicates that the problem is one of divine determination rather than her own sin or Abraham's impotence. She avoids using Hagar's name; "maidservant" renders the woman a commodity. She also indicates that Hagar's productivity, in all its manifestations, belongs to her, not Abraham. At this point in the story, Sarah has apparently insured if not enhanced her status. Whether she is viewed as acting altruistically, since the mother of the "great nation" promised to Abraham has not yet been named, or whether she demonstrates a lack of faith in the divine ability to allow her to conceive (consider the similarity of her delivering of Hagar to Abraham and Eve's delivering of the fruit to Adam [Gen. 16:3, Gen. 3:6]) will depend on the reader's perspective.[28]

The narrative context of this account further complicates any simplistic evaluation of Sarah. Her placing of Hagar in Abraham's embrace recollects what Abraham had done to her in the courts of Pharaoh and Abimelech.[29] She issues Abraham a command ("Go in to my maidservant"), and she provides the reason for it ("that I shall obtain children by her"). The language (Gen. 16:2) parallels the conversation the couple have prior to the descent to Egypt: Abram tells his wife (Gen. 12:13), "Say you are my sister" (command; possessive; relational object) "so that it will go well with me because of you, and that my life may be spared on your account" (rationale concerned with life and the future). Ironically, it may be that Sarah's misreading of future events, for she does not "obtain children" through Hagar, signals Abraham's error: we as readers are given no indication in Genesis that the Egyptians would have killed the husband in order to obtain the wife.

Whether Sarah's sojourn in the harem worked to her benefit is debatable, as is the comparable question of whether Hagar profited by becoming Abraham's wife. That Hagar finds self-expression after being given to Abraham and conceiving may suggest that Sarah's own situation of exploitation led to new self-determination. Only in Egypt does Abraham actually recognize Sarah's beauty and her worth.[30] Only in Egypt —not when he uproots his wife and nephew from Haran—does he finally talk with her. And perhaps first in Egypt does Sarah finally achieve some form of self-definition. As Fokkelien van Dijk-Hemmes observes concerning Gen. 12:17, the Hebrew expression *al d'var Sarai* need not mean only "on account of" Sarah (as it is traditionally rendered); it can also mean "because of the word of Sarah."[31] The narrative is not explicit as to whether Sarah and the Pharaoh had sexual relations (Gen. 12:19 is vague), let alone what Sarah might have wished for herself.[32] The parallel to Hagar in terms of sexuality is, at most, suggestive.

While van Dijk-Hemmes concludes that Sarah spoke to the deity, one could just as easily argue that she spoke her case to Pharaoh, who listened to her and so recognized Abraham's ruse. In turn, Sarah may well have been silent before Pharaoh. Traded by her husband, she may have had neither words nor anyone to hear them.[33] Commentators have variously explained her silence in terms of complicity, of victimization and powerlessness, and of survival.[34] Perhaps it is religious conservativism that prevents the suggestion that Sarah, tired of infertility in infertile Canaan, and tired of Abraham's perfunctory attitude toward her, actually appreciated her time amid the fleshpots of Egypt.

Complicit or not, Sarah and Hagar are both placed in sexual servitude by others. In each case, the giver appears in an ambivalent if not negative light. Although Abraham benefits financially from his willingness to allow Sarah to enter the harem, he is reduced in Pharaoh's eyes for his deception (Gen. 12:18–19). In like manner, while Sarah (the giver) expects to benefit by Hagar's giving birth, she loses status when this other Egyptian recognizes her own value.

The events that unfold forcefully depict the shifting of status positions between mistress and slave.[35] When Hagar conceives, "her mistress became light (*qll*) in her eyes" (Gen. 16:4). The reference has a twofold resonance: weighty in her pride and her pregnancy, Hagar clearly contrasts Sarah's lack. The Hebrew *qll* functions on at least two levels: first, it puns on the physical state of the two women, in that Hagar will become heavy with child while Sarah will remain light; second, it indicates that the hierarchical relationship between the two women has been reversed.[36] By "slighting" Sarah, Hagar, too, oppresses.

Sarah's reaction to the shift in status is immediate, but indirect. Rather than talk with Hagar, she again mediates the situation through her husband: "Then Sarai said to Abram, 'May the wrong done to me be on you! I placed my maidservant into your lap, and when she saw that she had conceived, I became light in her eyes. May the Lord judge between you and me'" (Gen. 16:5). Abraham places all responsibility back into Sarah's lap; she then so mistreats Hagar that the servant "ran from before her face" (Gen. 16:6b).

Just as Sarah utilized Abraham's lack of concern in order to oppress Hagar, so that same lack of concern manifests itself to her detriment in Gerar (Gen. 20). The parallels between the circumstances of the two women are reinforced by the connection among the terms Gerar, Hagar, and *la'gur* (to be a stranger, to sojourn).[37] Even though Abraham has by this time received the promise that Sarah would have a child, and even though it is quite likely that she is already pregnant,[38] he nevertheless announces to Abimelech that she is his sister and allows (encourages?) her placement in the harem. If Sarah is indeed pregnant, then her consignment to Abimelech's harem generates another parallel to Hagar: both women, while pregnant, remain apart from Abraham until they are sent back through divine machinations. (We might wonder if either wanted to return.) Both women, once returned, give birth to sons.

Symbolic resonances connecting these scenes of women in servitude and in danger to the later history of Israel enhance even as they complicate the biblical portraits of Sarah and Hagar. Genesis 12:17–20, which relates the departure of Abraham and Sarah from Egypt following the plagues and with the Pharaoh's gifts in tow, provides linguistic connections to the Exodus event.[39] Thus the matriarch prefigures the fate of her descendants in slavery and in liberation.

Hagar's slavery in contrast to Sarah's so-called freedom is reversed at the beginning of Exodus, in which the Egyptian Pharaoh enslaves Sarah's Hebrew descendants. Trible observes, "With a disturbing twist, the words of Sarah anticipate vocabulary and themes from the Exodus narrative. When plagues threatened the life of his firstborn son, Pharaoh cast out (*grs*) the Hebrew slaves. Like that monarch, Sarah the matriarch wants to protect the life of her own son by casting out (*grs*) Hagar the slave . . . Hagar continues to prefigure Israel's story even as Sarah foreshadows Egypt's role."[40]

The connections among women, ethnic markers, slavery, and pregnancy are even more intertwined. The Ishmaelites—descendants of Hagar—deliver Sarah's descendant Joseph in slavery to the Egyptian Potiphar (Gen. 37:28, 39:1).[41] At the time of the Exodus it is Hebrew slaves, not the Egyptian, who become pregnant and give birth easily (Exod. 1:19); now it is Hebrew slave women who risk seeing the death of their sons (Exod. 1:22, here from too much water rather than not enough; compare Gen. 21:16–19). Never meeting, Sarah and Hagar remain inextricably connected, through Abraham, through their own actions, through divine concern, and through symbolic representation.

Unlike the mothers, the sons do meet. Whether their encounter is initially for good or ill is, however, unclear. The problematic verse is Gen. 21:9. The NRSV translates with the Septuagint and the Vulgate, "But Sarah saw the son of Hagar the Egyptian, whom she had borne to Abraham, playing with her son Isaac." The Hebrew (MT) lacks the phrase "with her son Isaac." Much has been made of this text-critical problem, the term "playing" (*mitzacheq*), and Sarah's motivations. The Hebrew *mitzacheq*, which is from the same root as the name Isaac (*Yitzchaq*), conveys the sense of "laughter" and "playing" (or the quaint "making sport"); it is the same term found in Gen. 26:8, where Abimelech of Gerar witnesses Isaac engaged in some activity (the NRSV reads "fondling") with Rebecca. According to various citations in *Genesis Rabbah* (following the Hebrew text), the term variously means fornicating, committing idolatry, and murder. Thus Sarah protected her son from Ishmael's negative example.[42] Hackett suggests, given the connection of the verb to Isaac's name, that Ishmael was not merely "playing" but "Isaac-ing," and "this is perhaps what Sarah is complaining about in the next verse, that she noticed Ishmael doing something to indicate he was just like Isaac, that they were equals, and it is this that threatens her so."[43]

More benevolent readings are also possible. For example, the Greek and the Latin could be read as suggesting that Ishmael was expressing a form of playful closeness. The two boys may have been sharing an intimate but nonsexual moment (compare one reading of Isaac and Rebecca in Gerar) followed by Sarah's recognition that Ishmael will now play a new, major role in her son's life that she cannot. That the scene follows directly on the announcement that Isaac was weaned (Gen. 21:8) enhances Sarah's pathos. Faced first with Hagar's slight and now Ishmael's close relationship with her son, she finds herself impelled to remove both challenges to her own position and self-identity.[44]

Once Hagar and Ishmael are exiled from Sarah's sight, so too is Sarah exiled from the narrative. Her name is not mentioned again until Gen-

Sarah

esis 23:1–2, her death notice. Hagar's death is not recorded: while the authors of Genesis may have found this datum unimportant, the gap has substantial contemporary hermeneutical implications. Positively, Hagar's freedom and self-determination do not die. Negatively, neither do the threats that she has faced: slavery, abuse, thirst, and exile.

The boys will meet again following Abraham's death. Genesis 25:8–9 records that when "Abraham was an old man and full of years, and was gathered to his people, his sons Isaac and Ishmael buried him in the cave of Machpelah, in the field . . . that Abraham purchased from the Hittites." The reunion thus necessarily takes place in the presence of Sarah; she was already interred in the cave (Gen. 23:9). The pericope concludes with references both to the blessing of Isaac and to the fulfillment of the promise to Hagar: Ishmael's descendants and their activities encompass Genesis 25:12–18. They become "twelve princes, according to their tribes" (25:16) and so anticipate Isaac's grandchildren. Then Ishmael's death is recorded, and "he was gathered to his people" (25:17). Although Hagar was told that her son would live in enmity with his neighbors and his relatives (16:12), the narrative may belie the prediction. Just as Hagar overcomes servility to find independence, to cry out to the deity, and to choose a wife for her son, so her son overcomes the prediction of hostility to unite with Isaac in the burial of their father and to be united with his family at his death. Ishmael does live in conflict with his brothers (that is, the extended family; the NRSV's "alongside of" misses the nuance of the Hebrew *nafal*); and he is, like Cain, Lot, and Esau, the disinherited child, but the break from his father is not total. The sons consequently achieve the unity that continually eludes the mothers.

"And Isaac settled at Beer-lahai-roi" (Gen. 25:11). The son of Sarah moves to the site named by Hagar; the sons of Ishmael, "from Havilah to Shur" (Gen. 25:18), are neighbors. The relationship between the families is not one of enmity but apparently one of peace: "Esau went to Ishmael and took Mahalath, daughter of Abraham's son Ishmael, and sister of Nebaioth, to be his wife in addition to the wives he had" (Gen. 28:9;[45] compare 36:2, where she is called Basemath). The daughter thereby reunites, at least temporarily, the family of Abraham that had been divided by the mothers.

Yet even such positive notices change with the generations. While the daughters continue to unite the family, the sons threaten to pull it apart. Ironically, the sons of Ishmael unite with (most of) the sons of Isaac in the selling of Joseph. Yet again, however, the women of the families will serve to unite. Genesis 39:1 reads, "Now Joseph was taken down to Egypt, and Potiphar . . . bought him from the *Ishmaelites* who had brought him down there." Genesis 37:36 states that "the *Midianites* had sold him in Egypt to Potiphar." Thus, one could easily identify the Ishmaelites with the Midianites. The Midianites are then brought back into the family of Abraham at the time of the Exodus. Moses, a Hebrew raised in Pharaoh's household and so an individual who bears in his own narrative traces of Sarah's story, marries a Midianite woman, Zipporah (Exod. 2:21). The name of their first son, Ger-shom (literally, "stranger there"; Exod. 2:22), echoes the name of Ha-Gar (literally, "the stranger, the sojourner").[46] And Zipporah will save Moses' life and so contribute to the rescue of his people (Exod. 4:24–26).

As for Sarah's daughters, by extension Rebecca is the first to occupy this role. Not only does she marry Sarah's son, she also takes her place in Isaac's emotions. As Genesis 24:67 remarks, "Then Isaac brought Rebecca into his mother Sarah's tent. He took Rebecca, and she became his wife; and he loved her, and so Isaac was comforted after his mother's death." This resourceful woman ensures the posterity of the covenant community by arranging the substitution of Jacob for Esau. Sarah's symbolic daughter, like Sarah herself, takes fate into her own hands and moves when her husband fails. Through her, the community continues. And yet both women lose their beloved sons: Sarah's death notice occurs immediately after the account of the Akedah; Rebecca will never see Jacob, who must flee from his cheated brother's anger. In death, as in life, there is both good and bad.

Sarah's first female biological descendant is Dinah, the daughter of Jacob and Leah. Although better known for her rape by Shechem and the subsequent massacre of the Shechemites by her brothers, Dinah does manifest one independent action: Genesis 34:1 states that "Now Dinah, the daughter of Leah, whom she had borne to Jacob, went out to visit the women of the region." It is the daughter who attempts to break down tribal barriers.

It is unclear how Sarah and Hagar would have fared had they given birth to daughters rather than sons. Would Sarah expel Hagar for bearing a girl? Or would Abraham exchange his daughter for his own safety, as he did with Sarah, and as his nephew Lot did with his own virgin daughters? Would Sarah have valued a daughter, or is her concern less lack of a child than lack of sons? Would these daughters have inherited not the indecisiveness of Abraham but the direction and resourcefulness of their mothers? Would they have found the means for survival in oppression? Would they have made peace with other "women of the land"? Would Sarah's daughter be like Miriam, who leads her people to freedom? Would Hagar's daughter be like that daughter of Pharaoh,

who rescues a Hebrew child and raises him as her son? That such questions can be asked at least provides some indication that exploitation is X
not inevitable, that cycles of oppression can be broken, that silenced
individuals and groups may someday recover their voices in imagination if not in historical record.

Just as the stories of Sarah and Hagar are incomplete, just as the characters remain open to allegorical interpretation and empathic reclamation, so too this feminist study concludes not with an assertion pro-
claiming "this is what the text means" but rather with an invitation to
look for ever-new meanings. Sarah and Hagar, characters in scripture,
remain apart. But their sons, and their daughters, can and do come together in tradition to work for the common good. Respecting each X
other's cultures and beliefs while celebrating their own, responsive to
each other's needs while responsible to their own community's concerns, Christians, Muslims, and Jews, daughters of Sarah and Hagar,
may yet bring peace to the family of Abraham.

Notes

1. Consequently, the "scriptures and traditions" with which I am most familiar are those of synagogue and Church; this familiarity, and an unfortunate lack
of expertise in Islamic sources, are reflected in the present study.

2. This is especially the case for the canonical texts of Church and Synagogue,
given variant versions, unmarked textual accretions and elisions, lack of auto-
graphs, conflicting interpretations throughout the centuries, and so on.

3. From Torah, Nevi'im (Prophets), and Ketuvim (Writings), the three parts of
the "Jewish" Bible.   TANAKH pg 14

4. For both Marx and Engels, the inequality of relations between men and
women served as an indicator of the progressive or oppressive character of a
society or mode of production. Feminist analysis to some extent separated from
Marxist analysis when the latter tried to subsume women under the category of
class. Still debated is whether "woman" constitutes the universal, primary category of other to the normative "male," or if this division is historically and
culturally contingent. Depending on the society and the circumstances, the
regnant configuration may not be man/woman but rather Jew/Gentile, West-
ern/Eastern, saved/damned, have/have not, and so forth.

5. From womanist, *mujerista,* Asian, lesbian, and other voices come multiple
challenges to "feminism" perceived as an essentialist category explicitly concerned with Caucasian, American, and European middle-class values, interested
primarily in matters of sex/gender (rather than, for example, economics and
security), and implicitly reinforcing cultural imperialism. It remains to be seen
whether these challenges will construct themselves in opposition to "feminism"
and so lead to separate enclaves of special issues (with perhaps an attendant
weakening of political strength), or whether such critiques can unite both for the

process of liberation and to destabilize the feminist enterprise from complacency and narrowness. For a helpful theoretical discussion having direct relation to scripture and tradition, see Elisabeth Schuessler Fiorenza, "Transforming the Legacy of the Women's Bible," in *Searching the Scriptures,* ed. idem, vol. 1: *A Feminist Introduction* (New York: Crossroad, 1993), 1–21, as well as the essays in the collection.

6. On various strategies, see the discussions in Carolyn Osiek, "The Feminist and the Bible: Hermeneutical Alternatives," in *Feminist Perspectives on Biblical Scholarship,* A. Y. Collins, ed. (Chico, Calif.: Scholars Press, 1985), 93–105; Elisabeth Schüssler Fiorenza, *Jesus, Miriam's Child, Sophia's Prophet: Critical Issues in Feminist Christology* (New York: Continuum, 1994), 3–63; Claudia V. Camp, "Feminist Theological Hermeneutics: Canon and Christian Identity," in Fiorenza, *Searching the Scriptures,* 1:154–71; Mary Ann Tolbert, "Defining the Problem: The Bible and Feminist Hermeneutics," *Semeia* 28 (1983): 113–26; and many others from within the field of religion. Biblical interpretation has also benefited from approaches developed by feminist literary critics; see, for example, Judith Fetterley, *The Resisting Reader: A Feminist Approach to American Fiction* (Bloomington: Indiana University Press, 1978).

7. For reclamations and (re)interpretations of Jewish texts and traditions, all engaged with "feminism," see the different strategies of Judith Plaskow in *Standing Again at Sinai: Judaism from a Feminist Perspective* (New York: Harper and Row, 1990) and other works; Daniel Boyarin, *Reading Sex in Talmudic Culture* (Berkeley: University of California Press, 1993); Alicia Ostriker, *The Nakedness of the Fathers: Biblical Visions and Revisions* (New Brunswick, N.J.: Rutgers University Press, 1994); the classic edited by Susannah Heschel, *On Being a Jewish Feminist: A Reader* (New York: Schocken Books, 1983); and Blu Greenberg's sensitive dialogue between "orthodoxy" and "feminism," *On Women and Judaism: A View from Tradition* (Philadelphia: Jewish Publication Society, 1981). For Christian texts and traditions, see the diverse perspectives of Mary Steward Van Leeuwen, *After Eden: Facing the Challenge of Gender Reconciliation* (Grand Rapids, Mich.: Eerdmans, 1993); Rebecca S. Chopp, *The Power to Speak: Feminism, Language, God* (New York: Crossroad, 1989); Elizabeth A. Johnson, *She Who Is: The Mystery of God in Feminist Theological Discourse* (New York: Crossroad, 1992); and the various writings of Rosemary Radford Ruether, Letty M. Russell, and Elisabeth Schüssler Fiorenza. Instructive as well is the corpus of Mary Daly. To these lists could be added many more names and titles.

8. Citation from Jacob Neusner, *Genesis Rabbah: The Judaic Commentary to the Book of Genesis: A New American Translation,* 3 vols. (Atlanta: Scholars Press, 1985), 2:172 (discussion on p. 173); with explanatory notes from H. Freedman, *Genesis,* in *Midrash Rabbah.* Translated into English with notes, glossary, and indices. Edited by H. Freedman and Maurice Simon (London: Soncino Press, 1939, I–II). See also Jacob Neusner, *Genesis and Judaism: The Perspective of Genesis Rabbah: An Analytical Anthology* (Atlanta: Scholars Press, 1985), esp. 141–43.

9. Phyllis Trible, *Texts of Terror: Literary-Feminist Readings of Biblical Narratives*

(Philadelphia: Fortress Press, 1984), 8. On the more popular level, one finds less benevolent depictions that view Sarah as the white and/or Jewish mistress and Hagar as the black and/or Christian slave. Thus one must be careful to avoid having Trible's epitaph play out allegorically, such that Hagar becomes the Christ and Sarah the (Jewish) executioner.

10. Trible, *Texts of Terror,* 28.

11. Delores S. Williams, *Sisters in the Wilderness: The Challenge of Womanist God-Talk* (Maryknoll, N.Y.: Orbis Books, 1993), 4. I have not seen Diana L. Hayes's *Hagar's Daughters: Womanist Ways of Being in the World* (New York: Paulist Press, 1995); this volume appropriates the image of Hagar for, as the catalogue blurb announces, "Black women but [also] to all women—and men."

12. See the discussions by Neusner in the texts cited above, in note 8.

13. Williams, *Sisters in the Wilderness,* 4.

14. Specifically, allegory involves "three interpretative operations: the schematizing or reduction of the original text or tradition; the (often implicit) assertion of an essential connection between the two planes of meaning that constitute the allegory; and the elimination of alternative meanings": Elizabeth A. Castelli, "Allegories of Hagar: Reading Galatians 4:21–31 with Postmodern Feminist Eyes," in *The New Literary Criticism and the New Testament,* ed. Edgar V. McKnight and Elizabeth Struthers Malbon (Valley Forge, Pa.: Trinity International Press; Sheffield: JSOT Press, 1994), 231–32. The following brief discussion of allegory owes much to Castelli's conjoining of feminist theory, postmodern awareness, and observations on the Pauline allegory of Sarah and Hagar.

15. See the very helpful discussion of the Pauline allegory by Sheila Briggs, "Galatians," in *Searching the Scriptures,* ed. E. S. Fiorenza, vol. 2: *A Feminist Commentary* (New York: Crossroad, 1994), 218–36, esp. 223–25, 230.

16. See note 9 above. See also the brief discussion by Savina J. Teubal, "Sarah and Hagar: Matriarchs and Visionaries," in *A Feminist Companion to Genesis,* ed. Athalya Brenner (Sheffield: Sheffield Academic Press, 1993), 244, following Delores Williams. Ironically, the Pauline allegory can be seen as equating Jews with Hagar; thus Galatians' confessional distinction between Judaizer and Pauline Christian forges an ethnic alliance between Egyptian and Jew.

17. See Elsa Tamez, "The Woman Who Complicated the History of Salvation," in *New Eyes for Reading: Biblical and Theological Reflections by Women from the Third World,* ed. J. S. Pobee and B. von Wartenburg-Potter (Oak Park, Ill.: Meyer Stone Books, 1987), 5–17. Conversely, see Jon D. Levenson, *The Death and Resurrection of the Beloved Son: The Transformation of Child Sacrifice in Judaism and Christianity* (New Haven and London: Yale University Press, 1993), 93: "The command to 'submit to [Sarai's] harsh treatment' is shocking. It is the most pointed counterexample to the misleading overgeneralization, popularized by liberation theologians, that the biblical God is on the side of the impoverished and the oppressed, exercising, as a matter of consistent principle, a 'preferential option for the poor.'" For Levenson, the "fierce independence of the Ishmaelites will vindicate the humiliating thralldom of their matriarch's life" (p. 95). Consideration of both

the dangers of pregnancy and the dangers of reading abuse where none is actually mentioned then complicate Levenson's interpretation. The wilderness is a dangerous place to bear a child, as Hagar's second experience in the desert indicates. Further, the text is silent regarding the next thirteen-plus years. It is not known if Hagar faced ongoing abuse or, instead, maintained a position of respect as a self-determined individual, as Abraham's wife and as the mother of his heir. See Danna Nolan Fewell and David M. Gunn, *Gender, Power, and Promise: The Subject of the Bible's First Story* (Nashville: Abingdon, 1993), 47.

18. Sharon Pace Jeansonne, *The Women of Genesis: From Sarah to Potiphar's Wife* (Minneapolis: Fortress Press, 1990), 4.

19. Trible, *Texts of Terror*, 9.

20. Or the "Hebrews" (where the connection to Jews may or may not be made by author and readers). Kwok Pui-Lan, "Racism and Ethnocentrism in Feminist Biblical Interpretation," observes that "Hagar, a foreigner and a slave, was not given the full status of a wife in Hebrew society because she was not eligible. Both Hagar and Sarai were valued only as 'containers' of Abram's seed in their society" (in Fiorenza, *Searching the Scriptures*, 1:106–7). The article ignores Gen. 16:3, which states that Sarah gave Hagar to Abraham "as a wife," other examples in "Hebrew society" where Hebrew men marry foreign women (e.g., Joseph), legal pronouncements on marriages to slaves, and the many suggestions that the women are more than containers (e.g., their actions, recorded by these "Hebrew" authors, that are not connected to their status as vessels). The positive cultural identifications of which the author speaks are undermined by reductive history.

21. The concern for blame has recently preoccupied feminist scholars even as they recognize the limitations of such labeling. See, for example, Fewell and Gunn, *Gender, Power, and Promise*, chap. 1, "Shifting the Blame." Katheryn Pfisterer Darr, *Far More Precious Than Jewels: Perspectives on Biblical Women* (Louisville: Westminster/John Knox, 1991), 148 and 156, respectively, labels discussions of Hagar: "Who Is to Blame? A Modern Midrashic Perspective" and "Who Is to Blame? Feminist Perspectives on Hagar and Her Story." Presenting scholars ancient and modern who blame Sarah, Hagar, Abraham, the Deity, the narrator, and patriarchal ideology, Darr locates the limitations of such discussions.

22. Athalya Brenner, "Female Social Behaviour: Two Descriptive Patterns within the 'Birth of the Hero' Paradigm," in Brenner, ed., *A Feminist Companion to Genesis* (reprinted from *Vetus Testamentum* 36.3 [1986]: 257–73), generously claims that "Sarah enjoys her husband's steadfast love, while his attitude towards Hagar does not extend beyond natural kindness" (p. 208). However, Abraham's "love" is brought into question by his dealings with the Pharaoh and Abimelech, as well as by the lack of its explicit mention. Nor does he show Hagar much kindness; his concern is rather for his son, Ishmael. Brenner also argues that "the two women apparently share one overriding ambition: to supply a son and heir to their master." This is generous, since Hagar's view on this matter is never expressed. In retrospect her life may have been much more pleasant prior to the birth of the child.

23. Sarai is the character's original name; it is changed to Sarah (cf. the change from Abram to Abraham) by the Deity following the institution of the covenant community via the sign of circumcision (Genesis 17). For consistency, I have adopted the spelling "Sarah" except in direct quotations where "Sarai" appears. On Sarah's lack of background, see Jeansonne, *Women of Genesis*, 14–15; cf. Fewell and Gunn, *Gender, Power, and Promise*, 39, and the citation there to Phyllis Trible, "Genesis 22: The Sacrifice of Sarah," in *"Not in Heaven": Coherence and Complexity in Biblical Narrative*, ed. Jason P. Rosenblatt and Joseph C. Sitterson, Jr. (Bloomington: Indiana University Press, 1991), 183, on Sarah as a woman without past or future. Abraham asserts, quite abruptly, to Abimelech of Gerar that Sarah is his "sister, the daughter of my father but not the daughter of my mother, and she became my wife" (Genesis 20:12), yet his comment is not confirmed and is therefore questionable; see also David J. A. Clines, *What Does Eve Do to Help? And Other Readerly Questions to the Old Testament* (Sheffield: JSOT Press, 1990/94), 76. Moreover, as Devorah Steinmetz, *From Father to Son: Kinship, Conflict, and Continuity in Genesis* (Louisville, Ky.: Westminster/John Knox, 1991), correctly notes, "Even if, as some have suggested, Abraham's claim refers to a specific type of aristocratic marriage, the information, in this context, is irrelevant. It is irrelevant, too, if Abraham's claim is literally true. Sarah is still Abraham's wife, and Abimelek is not free to take her" (p. 65). On the identification of Sarah with Iscah of Gen. 11:29, see *Genesis Rabbah* parashah 38 (cf. 45) and Steinmetz, *From Father to Son*, 166–67n.17.

24. Parashah 45: "Said R. Simeon b. Yohai, 'Hagar was the daughter of Pharaoh. When he saw the wonderful deeds that were done for Sarah when she was in his house, he took his daughter and gave her to Sarai, saying, 'It is better that my daughter should be a servant girl in this household, rather than a matron in some other house.' That is in line with this verse of Scripture: 'She had an Egyptian maid, whose name was Hagar' (Gen. 16:1). The sense of 'Hagar' is, 'Here is your reward' [a play on the word for Hagar and for reward, *agar*]." Citation and discussion in Jacob Neusner, *Genesis Rabbah*, 146. See also the brief discussion in Darr, *Far More Precious*, 135.

25. The NRSV's "that I shall obtain children by her" loses the parallelism. On Abraham's using his wife to increase his economic worth, see Fewell and Gunn, *Gender, Power, and Promise*, 42–43.

26. On the threat to the patriarch rather than the matriarch in Genesis 12, 20, and 26, see Clines, *What Does Eve Do*, 67. Clines notes that the dangers are also of the patriarchs' making; so too for Sarah: the plan for surrogacy threatens her own status. While the fears of Abraham and Isaac were apparently groundless, Sarah expresses her concern for loss of position after the narrator describes her diminution in Hagar's eyes.

27. Brenner, "Female Social Behaviour," 207. The comment is pregnant with implications for contemporary groups who see themselves as related racially, ethnically, or otherwise to one character as opposed to the other.

28. For various interpretations, see Levenson, *The Death and Resurrection*, 90–

91. On the connection of chapters 16 and 3, Levenson follows Joel Rosenberg, *King and Kin* (Bloomington and Indianapolis: Indiana University Press, 1986).

29. Trible, *Texts of Terror*, 9, dismisses the recapitulative aspect of Hagar's situation: "To be sure, on two occasions Abraham betrays [Sarah], passing her off as his sister to protect himself (12:10–20; 20:1–19), but each time God comes to her rescue. Without effort, this woman along with her husband enjoys divine favor." The opposite of such a dismissal is the conclusion—noted by Jo Ann Hackett, "Rehabilitating Hagar: Fragments of an Epic Pattern," in *Gender and Difference in Ancient Israel*, ed. Peggy L. Day (Minneapolis: Fortress, 1989), 139—that many (male) commentators draw concerning Hagar's situation: it "would have been a great honor for such a woman to sleep with the patriarch." In each case, the woman's own lack of control over her body is disregarded. For more on the parallel, see Fewell and Gunn, *Gender, Power, and Promise*, 45. See also *Genesis Rabbah*, 45: "She drew her along with the persuasive words, saying to her, 'Happy are you, that you will cleave to that holy body.'"

30. The Babylonian Talmud (*BT Baba Batra* 16a) suggests that Abraham did not realize until that moment that Sarah was beautiful; preserving his chastity, he had never before looked at her directly. See Darr, *Far More Precious*, 95. More mundane is *Genesis Rabbah* (p. 40), which explains that Abraham's remark was prompted by Sarah's loveliness despite the travail of travel.

31. Fokkelien van Dijk-Hemmes, "Sarai's Exile: A Gender-Motivated Reading of Genesis 12.10–13.2," in Brenner, *A Feminist Companion to Genesis*, 231. See also Neusner, *Genesis Rabbah*, 89, for alternative readings of the scene.

32. On the narrative's silence concerning the consummation of the relationship between Sarah and Pharaoh, and the attendant fact that "what did or did not happen to Sarah in the royal harem receives more attention from scholars than it does from Abraham," see J. Cheryl Exum, "'Who's Afraid of the Endangered Ancestress'?" in *The New Literary Criticism and the Hebrew Bible*, ed. Exum and David J. A. Clines (Valley Forge, Pa.: Trinity International Press, 1993), 92–93 and notes. Exum's discussion of the scholarship concerning class, gender, and loss of honor is well taken.

33. Contrast Gen. 20:5; Abimelech of Gerar insists that Sarah also told him that she was Abraham's sister.

34. See the listings in Fewell and Gunn, *Gender, Power, and Promise*, 43. Jeansonne, *Women of Genesis*, 17, regards Sarah's silence in response to Abraham's plan as "not an indication of complicity, but rather a testimony to her powerlessness." Not unexpectedly, rabbinic sources have her praying for her rescue from Pharaoh. Conversely, Exum first notes the problem of the (literal) argument from silence, and then correctly states that "it too easily leads us into a victim-victimizer dichotomy that ignores women's complicity in patriarchy." For Exum, finally, Sarah "is an accomplice because her character is the creation of an androcentric narrator" ("Who's Afraid," 107 n. 33). The same questions of complicity, victimization, survival, and even celebration of the particular turn of events could also be applied to Hagar in her relationship with Abraham.

35. Hackett, "Rehabilitating Hagar," 13, posits a narrative assumption that it was Sarah's duty to provide a woman to bear a child for her husband: "That is to say, Sarai's society might actually force upon her loss of status, until the point where she herself would bear children." For a more positive, much more imaginative reconstruction, see Savina J. Teubal, *Sarah the Priestess: The First Matriarch of Genesis* (Athens, Ohio: Swallow Press, 1984), and Teubal, *Hagar the Egyptian: The Lost Traditions of the Matriarchs* (San Francisco: Harper and Row, 1990).

36. Hackett, "Rehabilitating Hagar," 12, suggests that such translations as "Hagar looked on Sarai with contempt" (RSV) or "she despised her mistress" (NEB) are too harsh. For Hackett, the import is that Sarah "became diminished" in Hagar's eyes. The harshness, however, is embedded in the irony: to be "heavy" is the one thing Sarah wants. See also Trible, *Texts of Terror*, 12–13.

37. Steinmetz, *From Father to Son*, 168 n. 26. The connection to *la'gur* recurs in the wilderness experience of the Exodus generation, commands that sojourners are not to be oppressed (e.g., Exod. 22:20 [21]), and the name of Moses' first son. See below on Zipporah and Gershom.

38. Clines, *What Does Eve Do*, 75, following Peter Miscall, *The Workings of Old Testament Narrative* (Philadelphia: Fortress Press, 1983), 32. See also Exum, "Who's Afraid," 96.

39. See Michael Fishbane, *Biblical Interpretation in Ancient Israel* (Oxford: Oxford University Press, 1985), 375–76, and, expanding on his observations, Levenson, *The Death and Resurrection*, 86, 100.

40. Trible, *Texts of Terror*, 21; cf. 13–14. Similarly, Sarah "afflicts" (*'nh*) Hagar (16:6b), just as the Egyptians will afflict (*'nh*) the Hebrews (Exod. 1:11, 12; Deut. 26:6); Hagar flees (*brh*) from Sarah's abuse just as the Hebrews will flee (*brh*) Egypt (Exod. 14:5a); both will flee to the wilderness; both will reach Shur. Expanding on the connection between Hagar and the Israelite slaves, Trible observes that "no deity comes to deliver [Hagar] from bondage and oppression." This contrast to Israel here is slightly overdrawn; no one came to deliver those first generations under slavery either. On the connections, see also Levenson, *The Death and Resurrection*, 95.

41. Trible states that Hagar's last act is to insure that her son's descendants will be Egyptian in that she chooses an Egyptian wife for Ishmael (*Texts of Terror*, 27). However, the text does not conform to this concern, since the descendants of Ishmael form their own tribal if not ethnic group: they are named in contradistinction to the Egyptians. Ethnic identification and therefore contemporary ethnic readings are more complex than is usually argued.

42. In *Genesis Rabbah* (p. 53), Rabbi Akiba interprets: "But Sarah saw the son of Hagar the Egyptian, whom she had borne to Abraham, making sport" (Gen. 21:9). The phrase "making sport" bears only one meaning, namely, fornicating, in line with this verse: "The Hebrew servant whom you brought me came into me to make sport of me" (Gen. 39:17). This teaches, then, that Sarah saw Ishmael seducing "gardens" [virgins], making love to married women and dishonoring them." Rabbi Ishmael connects the term to idolatry (cf. Exod. 32:6); Rabbi

Eleazar to murder (cf. 2 Sam. 2:15). Texts from Neusner, *Genesis Rabbah*, 253. See also the discussion in Darr, *Far More Precious*, 142–43.

43. Hackett, "Rehabilitating Hagar," 20–22.

44. Alternatively, contemporary Western fears of child abuse might also be read into this passage.

45. Cf. Gen. 36:3, where Ishmael's daughter is identified as Basemath; contrast Gen. 26:34, which identifies Basemath as the daughter of Elon the Hittite.

46. See Jeansonne, *Women of Genesis*, 11 (cf. pp. 44 and 126 n. 3), on how the name Hagar echoes *gur*, the "stranger" or "foreigner," and so appropriately "is associated with the woman who will never be integrated into Abraham's family." Conversely, it may be precisely as a "stranger" or "foreigner" that Hagar embodies Abraham's family, who themselves will be sojourners in Egypt. The name may also be connected with Hagar's attempted escape from Sarah: Hackett suggests that her name may "mean something like 'flight'" and that "it is the same root as is used of Muhammad's *Hijrah*." See Hackett, "Rehabilitating Hagar," 14. Similarly, Jeansonne, *Women of Genesis*, p. 126 n. 3, states that while the root *h-g-r* is unknown, there is an Arabic cognate meaning "forsake, retire."

2

Hearing Hannah's Voice

The Jewish Feminist Challenge and Ritual Innovation

Leila Gal Berner

An opportunity for Muslim, Jewish, and Christian feminists to come together in dialogue is a blessing, for it is a truism that when we hear the voice of an "other," we learn more about ourselves; when we learn about an "other's" journey, much about our own journeys becomes clearer to us.

As a Jewish feminist, I take one particular kind of feminist journey. I am a Jew who honors but does not consider herself bound by traditional *halakha* (Jewish law). Other Jewish feminists have elected to carve out a place for feminism in the ritual realm while remaining within the boundaries of traditional halakha.[1] Our approaches are quite different, but we share a commitment to giving voice to Jewish women's spiritual concerns, and shaping a Judaism for the future that incorporates women's voices and life experience as part of legitimate Jewish Tradition (with a capital "T"). *neat*

My comments will focus on ritual innovation characteristic of the way a significant number of contemporary American Jewish women have sought to add feminist content and values to the Jewish ritual heritage, a tradition conceived of and created exclusively by men.

to them—only gender that matters o's

For millennia, Israelite and Jewish women have cultivated a religious "folk" tradition replete with chants, songs, special recitations, and ritual objects such as amulets and prayer bowls. While kneading bread, or chopping vegetables, while giving birth and nursing their young, Jewish women called out to God, voices raised in supplication, dialogue, and communion.[2] Through the centuries, however, women's heartfelt voices raised in song and celebration have generally been ignored by the male shapers of Jewish tradition, who have been indifferent (and sometimes hostile) to acknowledging women's concerns and experiences as pertinent to communal prayer and Jewish ritual.

In the days of the first and early second Temple in Jerusalem, men and women celebrated and worshipped together. By the Talmudic era (fourth–sixth centuries C.E.), segregation was the norm.

This deepening gender segregation seems to be a logical outgrowth of the Talmudic-era rabbis' preoccupation with discerning divine purpose and justification for the destruction of the Jerusalem Temple in 70 C.E. and the subsequent exile of the Jewish people from the land of Israel. In attempting to explain the calamity that befell Jewish Jerusalem, the exiled rabbis increasingly focused on the traditional notion that each human being holds within her- or himself two warring proclivities, the *yetzer tov*, the impulse toward good, and the *yetzer ra*, the inclination toward evil, and that it is the latter that is the source of the people's collective calamity.

In interpreting the prophet Zechariah's description of the apocalyptic "Day of the Lord"[3] (in which good would ultimately triumph over evil), one Talmudic rabbi commented, about a time of celebration, that "[I]f in the future to come, when they will be engaged in mourning and the Evil Inclination has no power over them, the Torah says men apart and women apart, now that they are engaged in rejoicing and the Evil Inclination has power over them, all the more so" (should men and women be separated).[4]

In this regard, Rabbi Susan Grossman points out that "the concern with the Evil Inclination seems overriding. It sets a cultural context in which the [Talmudic-era] rabbis would have assumed that the separation of sexes, being a desirable method for overcoming the Evil Inclination, would have existed in the Temple."[5]

Thus, in response to their conclusion that the yetzer ra had triumphed over good, and brought about the fall of Jewish Jerusalem and the beginning of a collective exile, the Talmudic rabbis sought to legislate Jewish life more strictly so that the people's evil proclivities would more effectively be held in check. Within this increasingly rigid legislation, the view that men and women had historically been separated in the Temple "served to underlie all later decisions to segregate men and women, especially during prayer and other ritual events."[6]

As gender separation became increasingly enforced in Talmudic times, women's voices were dimmed, as they were relegated to more and more remote areas of the synagogue, distant from the center of religious activity. It became increasingly easy for the male shapers of Jewish liturgy to disregard women's voices altogether.

It is for this reason that I focus on a moment in the biblical narrative, the story of Hannah, who lived in the first Temple era (circa 1,000 B.C.E.), in which a woman's voice was still heard and still heeded. Hannah is the first woman mentioned in Hebrew scripture as raising her voice in prayer, the first woman to embody a new mode of communication between humans and God.

> Hannah rose and presented herself before the Lord. Now Eli the
> priest was sitting on the seat beside the doorpost of the Temple
> of the Lord. She was deeply distressed and prayed to the Lord,
> and wept bitterly. She made this vow, "O Lord of hosts, if only
> You will look on the misery of Your servant, and remember me
> and not forget Your servant, but will give to Your servant a male
> child, then I will set him before You. . . . As she continued
> praying before the Lord, Eli observed her mouth. Hannah was
> praying silently; only her lips moved, but her voice was not
> heard; therefore Eli thought she was drunk. So Eli said to her,
> "How long will you make a drunken spectacle of yourself? Put
> away your wine." But Hannah answered, "No, my lord, I am a
> woman deeply troubled; I have drunk neither wine nor strong
> drink, but I have been pouring out my soul before the Lord. Do
> not regard your servant as a worthless woman, for I have been
> speaking out of my great anxiety and vexation at this time."[7]

According to Jewish tradition, the first instance of what we now think of as "personal prayer" occurred when the childless Hannah spoke in a direct and intimate way to God, asking the source of all life for the gift of motherhood. So unusual was this form of religious devotion that Eli, the high priest, could not comprehend it. Never before had he seen anyone speak so personally with God, and he concluded that Hannah's strange behavior was due to intoxication.

Hannah's response to Eli's accusation is revealing. She tells him that she is speaking to God out of her own painful experience: "I am a woman deeply troubled; . . . I have been pouring out my soul before the

Lord. . . . I have been speaking out of my great anxiety and vexation at this time."

As Carol Gilligan pointed out in her landmark work, *In a Different Voice: Psychological Theory and Women's Development*,[8] men and women communicate differently, motivated by different social contexts. For females, Gilligan suggests, fluid, unrestricted relationships with others based on common experience and emotional connection is key, while for males a consensus-formed structure and framework (that is, a set of "rules") is central to relationships.

From this perspective, Hannah and Eli act in ways consistent with what Gilligan has identified as characteristic gender-related behavior: Hannah speaks as a woman to God out of her own very personal anguish. She prays in an unstructured way, sharing her emotional state of mind with God. Eli reacts as a man who naturally gravitates toward structure, that is, toward the ritual "rules" with which he is familiar and comfortable. This moment of conflict between Eli, a representative of the cultic "tradition," and Hannah, with her own idiosyncratic spiritual style, reflects a centuries-old reality: men and women experience and communicate with the Divine in very different ways. Here we encounter the crux of the feminist challenge to religious tradition.

A place must be carved out within tradition to acknowledge and accommodate a uniquely female experience of the Divine. Different ritual forms and formats must be created and woven into Jewish tradition so that voice may be given to varying modes of spiritual expression. Religious tradition must be open to acknowledging and affirming the very different ways in which men and women approach spirituality, theology, and prayer. New images for the Divine must be welcomed into the tradition, experimentation with new liturgical forms must be encouraged, and tradition must expand its liturgical repertoire to include and embrace ritual expression that reflects the uniqueness of women's and men's need to speak authentically with God.

Much of the feminist challenge to Jewish tradition has taken place on American soil in the past three decades. It is valuable to place our discussion in the context of the emerging feminist movement and of a consideration of the way feminism has impacted upon Jewish women and religious expression.

In the mid-1960s and 1970s, the feminist movement was most concerned with access to and inclusion within the traditional power structures of American society. Similarly, Jewish women, inspired by what has been called the secular "women's revolt"[9] of this era, sought equal access to Jewish institutions and ritual life.

One of the first salvos in American Jewish women's struggle for parity with men came in 1972, when a group of ten female members of a New York *havurah* (religious fellowship) attempted to be placed on the program of the upcoming convention of the Conservative Rabbinical Assembly. The convention chairman refused to reserve a time for the women to speak during the convention, stating that the program was already set, but that they could try again the following year. "But this was the 1970s," recalls Martha Ackelsberg, one of the group's leaders, "so we said 'to hell with you' and decided to go anyway."[10]

Calling the New York press, the women succeeded in having a story (complete with photos) printed about them in the *New York Post* on the day of their departure for the convention.

The group's agenda, outlined on a one-page flyer they distributed to the assembled rabbis (all male, since the Conservative movement had not yet taken up the question of female ordination), proposed an "equal access agenda" including rabbinical ordination for women and the appointment and election of women to leadership positions in synagogues and major national Jewish organizations.

In the realm of ritual life, the women (who by now had given themselves a group name, Ezrat Nashim, meaning "help for women"),[11] demanded that females be counted in the minyan, the quorum of ten required for communal prayer, and receive the honor of being called up to bless the Torah, a ritual distinction reserved for men.

Despite the convention chairman's rejection of their request to be placed on the program, the women were ultimately given room in which to speak—and it seems that they were in the right place at the right time.

In her 1996 book, *Taking Judaism Personally*, Judy Petsonk describes the group's experience at the rabbis' convention:

> A hundred rabbis showed up for one meeting. A hundred rabbis' wives for another. (The only slated activity for the wives was a fashion show.) . . . Some rabbis said calling women to the Torah would be the end of Judaism: men's lust would be aroused, and they would not be able to concentrate on prayer. But several rabbis said women in their congregations would be interested, and they asked to be put on *Ezrat Nashim*'s mailing list. One older woman stood and said, "Where have you been all these years? We've been waiting for this!" *Ezrat Nashim* began receiving letters from all over the United States, with many people asking if they could join the organization. But there was no organization, just ten women with chutzpah.[12]

The times were clearly ripe for change. Soon this small group of Conservative-Jewish feminists was transformed into a national movement that over the years has secured equal access for women in a variety of areas of Jewish life. Only a year after their first action, the Conservative movement voted to count women in the minyan, and eleven years later the first Conservative woman rabbi, Amy Eilberg, was ordained by the Jewish Theological Seminary.

Simultaneously with these events in the Conservative movement, progress in access to leadership was being made in the Reform denomination of Judaism. Indeed, in the same year that Ezrat Nashim was organized, Sally Priesand was ordained by the Hebrew Union College–Jewish Institute of Religion, the Reform movement's seminary.

Much Jewish feminist work in the 1970s also centered around halakha, Jewish religious law, and ways in which women might have access to, and be included more affirmatively within, the halakhic structure.

One of the pioneers in this area is Rachel Adler, who in 1973 wrote an important article entitled, "The Jew Who Wasn't There."[13] In it she demonstrated that halakha had historically excluded women from the social, cultural, and ritual life of the Jewish people. "Ultimately," Adler wrote, "our [Jewish women's] problem stems from the fact that we are viewed in Jewish law and practice as peripheral Jews."[14] Noting that in halakha, women, children, and slaves are forbidden to participate in many areas of ritual practice and "have limited credibility in Jewish law," Adler observed that only women can never transcend their circumscribed status: "only women can never grow up, or be freed, or otherwise leave the category" of limitation.[15]

At this point in the evolution of Jewish feminism, Rachel Adler and others who challenged the structures of halakha sought to repair, reinterpret, and expand the boundaries of the existing Jewish legal system in order to enfranchise women. Nonetheless (with the exception of Reform Jewish women, who reflected their denomination's general lack of interest in halakhic issues), most Jewish feminists never sought to go outside the structure of existing religious law. They continued to work with the components of a centuries-old structure, never challenging the efficacy of that structure.

It is within this context that the first work written by an Orthodox Jewish feminist, Blu Greenberg, was published, some nine years after the birth of Ezrat Nashim. Greenberg's book, *On Women and Judaism: A View from Tradition*, was "a sensitive attempt to reconcile the claims of feminists with complete observance of Jewish law." Greenberg's aim was to maintain halakha as the guiding structure of Jewish life, but to find ways within it to ameliorate women's status and expand their participation in Jewish institutional, ritual, and cultural life. Most of Greenberg's efforts still fell into the category of the "equal access agenda," and her work contributed little to a search for new or different structures for Jewish communal life.

During these "equal access, civil rights" years, much was accomplished: rabbinic ordination for Reform, Reconstructionist, and Conservative Jewish women, reconsideration and reinterpretation of many specific halakhot (Jewish statutes) to improve and enhance women's place within the tradition, introduction of feminist concerns into university Jewish studies curricula, and much more.

This progress, however, reflects only a symptomatic, "band-aid" approach; these changes did not address the more deeply *systemic* feminist challenge of "liberation" that lay beyond simple inclusion. As Judith Plaskow, a pre-eminent voice in contemporary Jewish feminism, observed in 1983, "The Jewish women's movement of the past decade has been and remains a civil-rights movement rather than a movement for women's liberation. It has focused on getting women a piece of the pie; it has not wanted to bake a new one!"[16]

In 1995 we found ourselves in the second generation of the Jewish feminist challenge. The issues that Jewish women had struggled with two or three decades earlier were less central to the Jewish-feminist agenda precisely because so much had been accomplished in terms of equal access.

The issues of the 1970s and 1980s have given way to new challenges in the 1990s and into the new century. Jewish feminists seeking to "bake a new pie" have progressed from a primary focus on access and inclusion to a concentration on deeper issues that cut to the core of Judaism. Many have come to realize that underlying the entire system of the male-created halakha is an assumption of women's "otherness," an assumption that if women's situation within Judaism is to improve, they must fit into a male-designed structure rather than that the structure should be reshaped to respond more authentically to women's needs as well as men's. As Judith Plaskow has observed in her landmark work, *Standing Again at Sinai: Judaism from a Feminist Perspective*, "underlying specific *halakhot* and outlasting their amelioration or rejection is an assumption [that] . . . men are the actors in religious and communal life because they are the normative Jews. Women are 'other than' the norm; we are less than fully human."[17]

In an important and poignant article published in 1985, Reconstructionist Rabbi Joy Levitt asks whether victories on the equal-access front are not just Pyrrhic victories.[18] Noting that the first generation of women rabbis felt compelled to emulate their male colleagues' "navy blue suit model," Levitt observed that some more radical women rabbis sought to push the pendulum far in the opposite direction by advocating a "Goddess model," in which they sought to discover the roots of ancient Israelite women's power in the fertility cults of the ancient Near East.

In seeking a more "integrated model," Levitt argues that female rabbis must liberate themselves from an internalized sense of "otherness" in which "normative" (to use Plaskow's word) means male. If this is indeed achieved, the entry of women into the rabbinate will not have been a Pyrrhic victory after all. Ultimately, the Jewish feminist struggle of our time centers around eradicating the deeply rooted historical Jewish notion that woman is "other," thereby restoring women's full humanity.

In this regard, let us return for a moment to Hannah's prayer and Eli's reaction. The reason that Eli was so puzzled and outraged by Hannah's devotional style was that it was so radically *outside* the Jewish "normative" mode of prayer of Eli's time. Hannah was doing something that had never been done before (at least, never officially or publicly as part of Jewish worship), and it did not fit into the male-conceived and -designed cultic ritual: it was profoundly "other."

Hannah's intimate conversation with God, and her bold defense against Eli's accusations, touch at the edges of the contemporary systemic challenge of Jewish feminism. I have my *own* way of speaking with God, Hannah tells Eli. I *am* free to pray in this way! I am (to use Plaskow's metaphor) baking a new pie. Similarly, Jewish feminists today make an equally bold statement: We have our *own* way of engaging with Judaism. And in approaching Judaism in our own way, we bring about our own liberation. The Jewish "pie" must be baked anew to combine the ingredients of a millennia-old tradition with a deep, contemporary feminist consciousness. What has been normative until now must be redefined and reconstituted to include within it both female and male perceptions of reality, both female and male experiences of religious life and spirituality.

So, how *do* Jewish feminists "bake a new pie?" Judith Plaskow is again most helpful in charting our course: "The need for a feminist Judaism," Plaskow states, "begins with hearing silence. It begins with noting the absence of women's history and experience as shaping forces in Jewish tradition. . . . Confronting the silence raises disturbing questions and stirs the impulse toward far-reaching change. What in the tradition is ours? What can we claim that has not also wounded us? What would have been different had the great silence been filled?"[19]

Hearing silence. This is our first (and most crucial) step in moving toward meta-level liberation for Jewish women. Contemporary Jewish feminism approaches the challenge of hearing the silence in a variety of ways.

First, much serious historical research is now being done to discover the lost voices of Jewish women who through the centuries contributed to our theological and devotional literature, who acted as communal leaders, and who helped keep alive a folk tradition of Jewish ritual observance alongside the official religion formulated and executed by men.[20]

A second way of hearing the silence is represented by the new exegetical work being done by women (and feminist men) to add to the corpus of Jewish midrash interpretive engagement with sacred Jewish texts. New questions are being asked about biblical stories and the women whose lives were so profoundly affected by events, yet whose voices are rarely heard as the narratives unfold. What did Sarah think, for example, when Abraham, himself perhaps "intoxicated" with God's word, takes Isaac, the child of Sarah's old age, up to the mountain of the Lord for sacrifice? What did Dinah think or feel after she was raped, and did she really want her brothers to slaughter all her rapist's male kin? What pain must Hagar have felt at her banishment into the desert with her son Ishmael? Did Sarah really want Hagar's death? What was Sarah really afraid of? Why was Miriam punished for demanding her rightful place of leadership alongside her younger brother, Moses? The questions are endless as women's life experiences, emotions, and responses are being woven back into the sacred text, rethreaded into the fabric of Jewish exegetical tradition.[21]

A third and very important way in which Jewish feminists are filling the "great silence" is by focusing attention on the personal and spiritual dimensions of Jewish women's life experiences. Rabbi Sue Levi Elwell has said that "Jewish women are writing the *new* Torah text with our own lives" (personal communication), meaning that our experiences as women, as Jews, and as human beings provide the new stories that inform and shape our evolving Jewish tradition. Thus, in addition to an increasingly rich feminist midrashic tradition, new and creative work is being done in the realm of Jewish ritual to incorporate and honor Jewish women's lives.

In "normative" (that is, male-designed) Jewish tradition, ritual serves a communal purpose, bringing together individual Jews for celebration and faithful devotion. Additionally, traditional Jewish life-cycle rituals honor the individual Jew at key moments: birth (Brith Milah/circumcision), adolescence (bar and bat mitzvah), marriage, and death. Beyond this limited repertoire, however, other significant transitional moments have not found expression in our ritual tradition. Where, for example, is the Jewish ritual sanctification of a young woman's emerging procreative power with the arrival of her menstrual cycle? Where is an *honoring* of, instead of a grieving for, the biological changes that occur for women at menopause? Where is a Jewish ritual acknowledgment of the pain and sadness of infertility, or the grief of miscarriage? And beyond the biological life cycle, where are the rituals that mark in a significant and spiritually compelling way the changing seasons of our lives, such as parent- or grandparenthood, adjustment to an empty nest, widowhood, or the transitions brought on by divorce, shifting professional realities, and other life circumstances?

Jewish women and men alike are in need of far more ritual acknowledgment and sanctification of key life moments. Rabbi Debra Orenstein points out in her 1994 book, *Lifecycles: Jewish Women on Life Passages and Personal Milestones,*

> feminist Jews have been instrumental in expanding the definition of life cycle in four ways: (1) By including women in the observance of passages that formerly spoke only to and of men— e.g., establishing Bat Mitzvah (for girls) along with Bar Mitzvah celebrations and covenant ceremonies for baby girls, along with those for boys; (2) by supplementing or altering traditional rituals related to life cycle—e.g., supplemental divorce rituals or alternative marriage contracts; (3) by valuing as sacred and sometimes ritualizing the events of women's biological cycle— e.g., menarche, menses, childbirth, miscarriage, menopause; and (4) by sacralizing non-biological passages and milestones not contemplated by the tradition—e.g., through ceremonies celebrating elder wisdom or healing from sexual abuse. In a sense, this listing occurs in ascending order of innovation. The first category adheres most closely to the tradition and seeks both parity and uniformity in communal observances. The last uses individual lives—not tradition—as its starting point and does not necessarily entail or expect community-wide norms.[22]

Each category of ritual innovation reflects the feminist orientation—to address the meta-level, systemic structure of Jewish ritual life.

In recent years, I have been deeply involved in the creation of new Jewish rituals with a feminist perspective. One such ritual is described in detail below. It emerged from the painful, real-life experience of a young woman whom I call Rachel, a victim of sexual abuse. Speaking at a workshop on spiritual healing, Rachel said,

> I am a survivor. I have endured the terror of a man who sexually abused me and forced me to keep the filthy secret. I have endured the shame, the near-annihilation of my soul, the terror of being touched, and the invasion of all my sacred spaces. Sometimes I feel as if I have gone through the Holocaust along with six million of my people. And each year, when those who have died are remembered, I consider it to be my day of remembrance as well. But unlike them, I am still alive. I have survived. I am strong, unashamed, and undefeated—and I want a celebration!

Rachel added that "for many years, I felt like a pariah, outside the tent of my people, in exile."[23]

A ritual for women survivors of sexual abuse, in particular, may serve to "gather in the exiles." For far too long, victims of sexual violation have been isolated or even banished because of a "dirty, shameful secret" that is not theirs. It is hard to acknowledge that sexual abuse happens within one's own community, and perhaps even harder for Jews who carry a pride of peoplehood based on exemplary ethical behavior. Yet we Jews must acknowledge the dark side that resides among us. When the Jewish community engages in collective denial, the victims remain in spiritual and emotional exile.

When we welcome survivors of sexual abuse home from exile, we ease their aloneness and affirm their place within the collective Jewish family. We also offer a clear and unequivocal message that a sexually abused Jewish woman is not a pariah, cut off from the life of her people, for she bears no responsibility for the abuse. Any ritual becomes more compelling if it is deeply rooted in the authentic experience and feelings of its participants, and if it resonates authentically with the sacred text, liturgy, language, music, and modes of ceremonial expression of the faith tradition from which it emerges. In short, a ritual "feels" Jewish if it reflects Jewish cadences, textures, and prayer modalities. A new ritual that resonates in this way with ancient Jewish ceremonies has a better chance of standing the test of time and becoming part of an evolving liturgical tradition.

This is what I have attempted to accomplish in the ritual described below.[24]

A Ritual for Healing from Sexual Abuse

Step 1: Creating supportive space. A circle of women gather around the woman for whom the ritual is being enacted (hereafter referred to as the "focus" woman). She begins with the word *hineni*—"here I am"—the Hebrew word Abraham used when God called to him and instructed Abraham to sacrifice his beloved son Isaac.[25] The focus woman acknowledges her aloneness, and the depth of her pain, the uniqueness of her anger. She is reassured by her friends that she is no longer alone. With the use of the word *hineni,* a famous and charged word for Jews acquainted with the story of the binding of Isaac, there is a hint that in the abuse she suffered, the woman was an innocent victim, just as Isaac was an innocent tool of God's testing of Abraham.

Everyone present sings a Hebrew song attributed to Reb Nachman of Bratslav, one of the greatest of the Hassidic masters. *"Kol ha-olam kulo gesher tzar me'od"*—"all of this world is a very narrow bridge"—and the main point is not to fear at all. These words help to create a contemplative mood through a traditional Jewish musical form, the traditional Hassidic melody.

Step 2: Acknowledging anger. A survivor's poem is read,[26] and the focus woman speaks of her own anger. She is given free rein to express the full range of her emotions. In response, her friends assure her that she is "loved by an unending love"—God's love. The words her friends speak are from an interpretive version by Rabbi Rami Shapiro of the traditional Ahavah Rabbah prayer: *ahava rabbah ahavtanu Adonai eloheinu*— "with abounding love, You have loved us, Adonai, our God."[27]

Step 3: Survival and gratitude. The focus woman reads from Psalm 147:3, "The Holy One heals the broken in heart and binds their wounds," and she continues: "I have survived a sad journey—with peril to body and soul. I thank You, God, for sustaining me and bringing me through the peril in wholeness." Here she reads or sings (in Hebrew or English, as is comfortable for her) a new musical version of the traditional Birkat ha-gomel prayer, in which one thanks God for helping to sustain one through danger: "I shall bless the Source of Life who fashions good and evil. I shall bless the Holy One who brings dark and light to all people. For I have walked in the valley of the shadow of death, and You, and you were with me then with every painful breath."

In this new prayer, traditional resonances abound. First, reference is made to the Yotzer blessing in the Sabbath liturgy that speaks about God's creation of dark and light. Second, reference is made to Isaiah 45:7, in which God is described as *yotzer tov u-voreh rah* (the one who fashions good and creates evil). Third, Psalm 23 is echoed ("yea, though I walk through the valley of the shadow of death, I will fear no evil, for You are with me"), and finally the new prayer echoes the Modeh Ani, a meditation recited by observant Jews upon awakening that is based on the Babylonian Talmud, Tractate Berakhot 60b: "I thank You, living and eternal God, for restoring my soul to me in compassion."

Step 4: Seeking healing. The focus woman's friends encircle and embrace her, and chant (in a mantra-like fashion) Moses' poignant prayer for his sister Miriam's healing (based on Numbers 12:13)—"*El na refana la, El na refana la*" ("Please God, heal her.")

As the chanting subsides, the group sings a musical adaptation of the Mi-sheh-beirach, the traditional prayer for healing:[28]

> *Mi sheh-beirach imoteinu, mekor ha-bracha l'avoteinu—*
> (May the One who blessed our mothers, source of blessing to our fathers)
> May the source of strength
> Who blessed the ones before us,
> Help us find the courage
> To make our lives a blessing—and let us say, amen.
>
> *Mi sheh-beirach imoteinu, mekor ha-bracha l'avoteinu—*
> Bless those in need of healing
> With *refuah shleymah,*
> The renewal of body,
> The renewal of spirit—and let us say, amen.

Step 5: Self-affirmation. The words spoken by the focus woman are taken directly from the traditional Jewish morning liturgy (based on the Babylonian Talmud, Tractate Berakhot 60b): "*Elohai neshama sheh-natata bi tehorah hi*"—"My God, the soul you have given me is pure. You created it, You formed it. You breathed it into me."

The focus woman continues: "I know that I am created *b'tzelem Elohim* (in the image of God), that a divine spark resides within me. *Hineni:* here I stand, no longer alone, on my way to becoming fully unafraid, knowing that I can create safe space for myself, knowing that I have a circle of loved and loving ones who will support and protect me, knowing that I am sheltered beneath the wings of the *Shekhina,* knowing my own power."

Here the focus woman expresses her direct connection to the Shekhina, the traditional name for the in-dwelling presence of God, associated with the feminine aspect of the Godhead. She concludes with a final prayer (taken directly from the daily dawn blessings, which are based on the Babylonian Talmud, Tractate Menakhot 43b): "*Baruch ata Adonai, sheh-asani isha, Baruch ata Adonai sheh-asani bat horin*"—"I bless You, Holy One, who has made me a woman. I bless you, Holy One, who has made me free." This affirmation is particularly empowering since in the traditional "normative" liturgy, only a man was expected to recite the dawn blessings in which he specifically thanked God for *not* making him a woman: "*sheh lo asani isha.*" The ritual concludes with a moment of silent reflection—and embraces.

And so I return to where I began, with Hannah and the deepest devotions of her heart. I am convinced that were she with us now, she would rejoice in the journey her Jewish sisters have taken. I am convinced that she would delight in the emerging new possibilities for her own spiritual expression. And perhaps even Eli would not be so astounded to see a woman praying to, and directly talking with, her God. In our time, in a Judaism powerfully informed by feminism, the silent season of Hannah's own experience, the pain of her infertility, would find eloquent and empathic expression.

A final desideratum, a final prayer: May the time come, speedily and in our days, when every season and every purpose under heaven in Jewish women's (and men's) lives will be embraced by an evolving Jewish tradition. May the time come, speedily and in our days, when the seasons of Jewish women's lives will no longer be silent and when the most profound moments of our life experiences will no longer be absent from the liturgical repertoire of the Jewish people.

Notes

1. See, for example, Blu Greenberg, *On Women and Judaism: A View from Tradition* (Philadelphia: Jewish Publication Society, 1981).

2. For information on Jewish women's folk religion, see Susan Grossman and Rivka Haut, eds., *Daughters of the King: Women and the Synagogue* (Philadelphia: Jewish Publication Society, 1992); Susan Starr Sered, *Women as Ritual Experts: The Religious Lives of the Elderly Women of Jerusalem* (New York: Oxford University Press, 1992); and Dianne Ashton and Ellen Umansky, eds., *Four Centuries of Jewish Women's Spirituality* (Boston: Beacon Press, 1992). See also Nina Beth Cardin, ed., *Out of the Depths I Call to You: A Book of Prayers for the Married Jewish Woman* (Livingston, N.J.: Jason Aronson, 1992).

3. Zechariah 12:12.

4. Babylonian Talmud, Tractate Sukkah 51b.

5. Susan Grossman, "Women in the Jerusalem Temple," in Grossman and Haut, *Daughters of the King*, 29.

6. Ibid.

7. 1 Samuel 1:9–16, *The Harper Collins Study Bible* (NRSV) (New York: Harper Collins, 1993).

8. Cambridge, Mass., Harvard University Press, 1993.

9. Jacob R. Marcus, *The American Jewish Woman, 1654–1980* (New York: KTAV Publishing House, 1981), 149.

10. Quoted in Judy Petsonk, *Taking Judaism Personally* (New York: The Free Press, 1996), 106.

11. The group's name contained a clever double entendre, since the term *ezrat nashim* was also the traditional name for the women's section in the courtyard of the ancient Temple in Jerusalem and was also used historically to indicate the section of the synagogue in which women were segregated from men.

12. Petsonk, *Taking Judaism Personally*, 107.

13. Adler, "The Jew Who Wasn't There: *Halakhah* and the Jewish Woman," *Response* 7, no. 22 (Summer 1973): 77–82, reprinted in *On Being a Jewish Feminist: A Reader*, ed. Susannah Heschel (New York: Schocken Books, 1983), 12–18.

14. Adler, "The Jew Who Wasn't There," in Heschel, *On Being a Jewish Feminist*, 13.

15. Ibid.

16. Judith Plaskow, "The Right Question Is Theological," in Heschel, *On Being a Jewish Feminist*, 11.

17. (San Francisco: Harper, 1990), 224.

18. Levitt, "Women Rabbis: A Pyrrhic Victory?" *Reconstructionist* 50, no. 4 (Jan.–Feb., 1985): 19–24.

19. Plaskow, *The Right Question*, 1.

20. See footnote 1 above.

21. For recent examples of feminist Jewish *midrash*, see Judith Antonelli, *In the Image of God: A Feminist Commentary on Torah* (Northvale, N.J.: Jason Aronson, 1995), and Ellen Frankel, *The Five Books of Miriam: A Woman's Commentary on the Torah* (New York: G. P. Putnam's Sons, 1996).

22. Orenstein, ed., *Lifecycles* (Woodstock, Vt.: Jewish Lights Publishing, 1994), xviii.

23. Workshop for survivors of sexual abuse, Philadelphia, 1991, transcript of tape-recorded session.

24. A caveat: the ritual's "feel" and mood cannot be adequately communicated in writing. One must actually experience the ritual in its fullness, in the authentic context of a healing moment.

25. Genesis 22:1 and 22:11.

26. See poem by Marta Metz in Leila Gal Berner, "Our Silent Seasons," in Orenstein, *Lifecycles*, 133–34.

27. In the traditional Jewish prayer book, preceding the central declaration of faith, "Sh'ma Yisra'el" (Hear, O Israel, the Lord our God, the Lord is One).

28. This contemporary version is by Debbie Friedman.

3

The Influence of Feminism
on Christianity

ALICE L. LAFFEY

Ordination

Although Antoinette Brown was ordained in the Congregational Church in 1853, and Louisa Woosley in a southern Presbyterian Church in 1889, it was not until 1955 that northern Presbyterians approved the ordination of women to the full ministry. One year later the Methodist Church voted to give women full status—ordination and membership in the Conference. In 1970 the Lutheran Church of America and the American Lutheran Church voted to ordain women. And in the Episcopal Church, in spite of the fact that eleven women were ordained in 1974, it was not until 1977 that a canon law went into effect that authorized the ordination of women. At the time of this writing, neither the Roman Catholic nor the Orthodox Church ordain women and no policy change in this regard is foreseen.[1]

The exclusion of women from ordination brought attention to the exclusion of women from theological education. Women could not be ordained because women were not theologically prepared, or so the argument went. But why were women not theologically prepared? Because women had been excluded from theological education. The equal rights approach succeeded in introducing women into theological schools. Many women students of theology quickly recognized that the scriptures and their interpretation as well as practices derived from the scriptures were permeated with patriarchy.

Theological Deconstruction and Reconstruction

In the final decades of the twentieth century, women not only won access to theological education but they achieved ordination and produced a host of theological materials on subjects ranging from women's ordination to feminist hermeneutics. The impact of their work has been far reaching.

Perhaps the first voice to challenge traditional expressions of theology was that of Mary Daly, a former Roman Catholic professionally associated with Boston College. Her *Beyond God the Father: Toward a Philosophy of Women's Liberation* (1973) was followed by *The Church and the Second Sex* (1985).[2] Though originally hired in the Department of Theology, Daly describes her work, because of its methods and its challenge to traditional theology, as philosophical and linguistic. She describes herself as post-Christian. Mary Daly represents one feminist response to Christianity, thoroughly imbued as it is with patriarchy: she has gone beyond, rejecting it.

Although Daly is not alone in her rejection of Christianity, neither is her response shared by all feminists. Many have chosen a more moderate course. Attempting to understand the historical origins and nature of patriarchy, many feminists work to distance the past from the present and to expose the patriarchal character of the biblical texts and later traditions in order to prevent the transmission of patriarchal biases into the present interpretations.[3]

One such Christian feminist is Rosemary Ruether, who, between 1967 and 1995, wrote and edited more than twenty books, most having to do with women and religion. In 1974 she edited *Religion and Sexism: Images of Women in the Jewish and Christian Traditions.*[4] In a series of complementary articles written by such feminists as Phyllis Bird, Constance Parvey, and Eleanor McLaughlin, the book exposes the Old Testament images of women, the Church Fathers' understanding of "virginal feminism," and medieval theology's assertion that while women's sex is not equal to men's, their souls are! These articles helped to lay bare the patriarchal biases inherent in the Judeo-Christian tradition. A year later Ruether published *New Women, New Earth: Sexist Ideologies and Human Liberation.*[5] With this book Ruether not only exposes sexism, she calls for human liberation.[6] Ruether then produced *Women-Church*, which sets forth a theology and practice for feminist liturgical communities.[7] In 1992 the recognition of sexism, the effort to replace sexist ideologies with human liberation, and the expression of women's religious equality in liturgical celebration, took another step forward with the publication of her eco-feminist theology of earth healing.[8]

Ruether's intellectual journey in religion and feminism is shared by many feminists who, though not as prolific or as well known as she, have nevertheless struggled to deconstruct the patriarchal paradigm in the scriptures and tradition, to construct and ritualize a liberating theology, and to act upon their evolving consciousness of the relationship of human liberation to cosmic healing and well-being.[9]

Scriptural Deconstruction and Reconstruction

At the same time that women theologians were challenging traditional theology, women biblicists were challenging scriptural interpretation. Perhaps the best-known Christian feminist to address the patriarchal nature and interpretation of the Old Testament is Phyllis Trible. Her first monograph, *God and the Rhetoric of Sexuality*, uses a literary-critical methodology to interpret texts. Her nontraditional but text-grounded interpretations suggest that she considers traditional interpretations to have been done from a patriarchal perspective.[10] Her second monograph uses the same methodology but with a different outcome. Her interpretations of Hagar, Tamar, and Jephthah's daughter in *Texts of Terror* expose how truly terrible certain biblical texts are.[11]

Many Christian women who are Old Testament scholars have deconstructed and reconstructed the biblical texts, especially but not exclusively those dealing with women. In 1994 Alice Ogden Bellis published *Helpmates, Harlots, and Heroes*, a volume that presents the commentary of many feminist biblical scholars on women in the Old Testament and includes a large bibliography.[12]

No one has more effectively challenged Christian New Testament scholarship than Elizabeth Schuessler Fiorenza. The author of some fifteen books, she published six monographs between 1983 and 1993 that have had revolutionary effects on Christian biblical scholarship. *In Memory of Her* puts a historical-critical methodology at the service of feminist concerns, showing the constraints placed on Christian women under Roman household codes and exposes the patriarchal tendencies of the early Church by her reconstruction of the evolving tradition regarding the woman who anointed Jesus.[13] In *Jesus in Bread, Not Stone* Fiorenza developed a feminist liberation hermeneutics;[14] and by 1992, when she published *But She Said*,[15] her feminist hermeneutics had become multiracial and multicultural.[16]

By 1992 Carol Newsom and Nancy Ringe had edited *The Women's Bible Commentary*, to which forty-two women biblical scholars contributed.[17] Although the volume focuses primarily on women and sexism, a new series of biblical commentary that Fiorenza herself has edited incorporates a more inclusive feminist hermeneutics.[18] At the popular level one now sees the recognition of patriarchy incorporated into many biblical teaching materials.[19]

Finally, the effect of feminist biblical interpretation has also been felt in private Bible reading and in communal liturgical celebration. Many people today pray with, and many churches have adopted, new translations of the Bible that use gender-inclusive language.[20]

A Feminist Biblical Reading: Vashti

To illustrate the reading of a biblical text from a feminist perspective, to suggest how feminist readings might differ from traditional interpretations, and to offer a concrete embodiment of assumptions and approaches used by some contemporary daughters of Sarah, I include here a reinterpretation of Esther 1:1–2:4, particularly as the passage affects the character of Vashti. The interpretive strategy includes close reading and honors a character that many might consider minor and inconsequential. While the reading employs a liberation perspective, a hermeneutics of suspicion, and a hermeneutics of imagination, it does not challenge the authority of the received text. Rather, the interpretation provided here illustrates how the social location of a decentered interpreter can shift the reader's focus and provide a biblical reading that challenges assumed power relations. Note how the reclaiming of Vashti decenters Queen Esther.[21]

Chapter 1 of the Book of Esther opens with a banquet hosted by King Ahasuerus for the nobles of his kingdom. The banquet lasts some 180 days and is followed by a banquet for the inhabitants of the capital that lasts 7 days. The text describes, in addition to the duration of the festivities, the number of persons involved, the luxury of the feast, the golden goblets, the abundance of royal wine, and the rich adornment of the chambers. Nothing has been spared. A comment is made that drinking took place "according to the law, no one was compelled" (1:8; RSV). Each man was free to indulge as he saw fit.

Then, almost as a parenthesis, verse 9 comments that Queen Vashti also gave a banquet for the women. Was it customary that the queen eat with the king and celebrate with him? Why this sexual separation? Was her banquet for the sake of the other women? Sources suggest that, according to Persian custom, the queen usually did eat with the king but that she left before the drinking and revelry commenced, whereas the concubines and the harem women stayed. Verse 9 continues with the location of the queen's banquet: in the palace that belonged to King Ahasuerus. Palaces belonged to kings and houses belonged to fathers (see, for example, Esther 4:14); although Vashti could give a banquet, she was dependent on the king, including for its location.

Historical critics have struggled to determine the number and duration of the banquets. Was there one banquet, or were there two? Did one last a full 180 days and the other only 7?[22] Whatever the number of banquets and whatever their duration, the text is clear that sufficient time was spent celebrating for the king's heart to be merry with wine (1:10).[23] The text of Esther emphasizes the men's condition by pointing out that it was the seventh day. There can be no doubt that many of the men were inebriated.[24]

Seven eunuchs who serve the king (1:10) are ordered to bring Queen Vashti before the king with her royal crown, to show the princes and the people her beauty (1:11). The king's intent seems to be to display the grandeur and beauty of his possessions. He owned the queen's crown and he possessed the queen; he was proud of his possessions and desired to show them off. A lesser amount of alcohol might have sharpened his judgment and avoided the attempted display, but it was the seventh day of a very sumptuous banquet. The author of the text emphasizes that Vashti was fair to behold, perhaps intending to justify the king's command (it was not a request) or at least to win a bit of sympathy and understanding from his male audience.

Only one half of one verse depicts Vashti as the subject of any action. The narrator, not Vashti, says quite straightforwardly, "But Queen Vashti refused to come at the king's command conveyed by the eunuchs" (1:12a).[25]

Up until this point in the account, all has been narration; there has been no direct address, no dialogue. The first to speak is King Ahasuerus, and those spoken to are the wise men, they who "see the king's face."[26] Ahasuerus asks a simple question: "According to the law, what is to be done to Queen Vashti because she has not performed the command of King Ahasuerus conveyed by the eunuchs?" (1:15). There has been one act of disobedience; there is one disobedient person, who happens to be a wife; there is one person disobeyed, who happens to be a king, or is he rather a king who happens to be a husband? A wife has disobeyed an edict of her king. Ahasuerus asks if there is a law to deal with such a situation. The king is represented here and elsewhere in the narrative as most law abiding.[27]

The next to speak, the one who answers the king, is Memucan, one of the wise men. His concern is not Vashti particularly; rather, he is concerned with the relationship between all men and all women. He uses Vashti for his own and all men's self-interest. Vashti, he says, has wronged not only the king but all the princes and all the peoples in all the provinces. He fears that all women will learn what the queen did, and that it will cause them to look with contempt on their husbands (1:17). Vashti will become their heroine and model. Memucan fears that even the princesses of Media and Persia will rebel against the princes.[28]

Having drawn a scenario abhorrent to most men, Memucan suggests a drastic, but seemingly necessary, solution. A royal edict has this law-abiding king create a law to be written among the laws of the Persians and the Medes.[29] This royal edict would proclaim that Vashti was not to come again before the king. The true purpose of this edict, however, seems clear; according to Memucan's own testimony, the edict was meant to guarantee that all women, high and low, would honor their husbands.

The king doesn't speak again. The narrator informs us that Memucan's advice pleased the king, who carried it out.[30] The king sent letters to all the provinces, to every province in its own script, to every people in its own language, that every man was to be lord in his own house (1:22). In this obviously hierarchical narrative—note the categories of people mentioned, including eunuchs, wise men, princes, servants, military men, nobles, governors, and ladies—making a husband prince[31] in his house intensified the normal patriarchal relationship and raised the husband's status over his wife even more than was customary.[32] Moreover, every man was to speak according to the language of his people. In contrast to the usual situation in families whereby, if the mother and father spoke different languages, the mother's language would prevail in the home and become the language of the children, Ahasuerus' edict reasserted the father's authority by making his language dominant in the home.[33]

While many modern commentators understand Chapter 1 as a fictionalized device to explain why the Persian queen was dethroned and to pave the way for the Jewess Esther to replace her, one must ask why, then, the narrative is so detailed. Why did the punishment not fit the crime? Yes, Vashti was removed, but her dismissal seems almost parenthetical. Just as her refusal of the king's command took only half a verse, the notice that she is to come no more before the king is equally brief (1:19b).

One cannot help but question what else is happening in Chapter 1. Is the author a lover of hyperbole for its own sake? Is the audience meant to suspect that Memucan's wife is a shrew? Are we to conclude that Memucan is the really drunk character who seizes the stage and the limelight with a vicarious display of power? Is it perhaps true, as many commentators have suggested, that the episode is filled with irony and humor? Why else would the wise men of the kingdom, those who know the times and who are versed in law and judgment, be called upon to settle a domestic dispute? On the other hand, the wise men, those "next to the king," had also been partying for a long time and were probably feeling no pain. I submit that the king would have been very angry with Vashti precisely because she had publicly, in front of those whom the king's male ego had wanted to impress, humiliated him by her refusal.

Might a contemporary reader legitimately wonder whether, in the world outside the text, there was a potential rebellion at hand? Just as persecution of the Jews is concentrated in the character of Mordecai (3:6), might a women's rebellion be centered in Vashti? Could there have been reason to fear that women, at least some, dissatisfied with the roles that patriarchal culture had assigned them, had begun to question and even to resist? Is the audience of the Book of Esther able to conclude that Vashti was also a bit tipsy from her banquet and that, consequently, her inhibitions were lessened as well as her fear, allowing her to express her true feelings? If this were the case, that the hierarchical relationship between the sexes was under stress at the time this narrative was developed, Vashti may well have been depicted not as a model to follow but rather as a model of what happens to women who do rebel: they are cast off! Heard in this light, her story becomes an opportunity to reaffirm the tradition that women are the possessions of their men and that husbands are their wives' lords.

This closer look at the character of Vashti forces one to ask if Esther is truly a heroine. She is the woman who plays the man's game. Not only does she submit to the beauty contest, she actively participates (2:10, 2:15). Esther carefully follows Hegai's advice on how to accentuate the positive and become the sex object par excellence. Body beautiful (2:2–3, 2:7) and successful sex (2:14) are her tickets to moving up in the world. Esther does not stand with her sister and protest the victimization to which Vashti had been subjected and that might lie in her future as well (2:14); rather, she accepts the rules of the dominant culture and works them to her advantage. She prepares her body for a full year (2:12) to win for it male approval.

This reading of the text suggests that Esther is not the heroine but a victim. She is the stereotypical female who exerts a great deal of effort to produce a beautiful body. She competes against other women for a man.

The normal routine of Esther's life becomes either to come or to stay away at her husband's pleasure. Esther is the product of a patriarchal culture, and from that culture's perspective she is a success.

The interpretations of Vashti and her nonaction are as varied as the perspectives of the people who would judge her. In my own interpretation, and in contrast to Esther, Vashti is truly the heroine. She risks almost certain yet unknown punishment to do what: to disobey her *ba'al*, her master and lord, her husband; to assert her own identity and decision-making potential; to preserve her dignity and self-respect. Vashti listens to her own best self; she acts autonomously and authentically; her authority is validated by internal standards, not by mere law-and-order claims of the society. In patriarchal cultures refusal to obey one's husband might well be judged an offense, and a woman immersed in that culture who deviated from its dictates might well feel guilt, and expect and receive punishment. In contrast, Vashti rises above that culture to hear the god, whether Persian or Israelite, who speaks in her own soul.

An Eco-Feminist Biblical Reading: The Ass

The narrative of Num. 22:21–35 includes an ass as one of the major characters.[34] The narrative is deliberately and carefully ambiguous about the status of the ass. She is an animal, not a human being;[35] yet she speaks, unlike asses but like human beings; and the behavior of this ass is superior to that of the human being to whom she speaks.

Verse 22 opens the literary unit, reasserting what verse 21 has already implied: the prophet Balaam is going to visit Balak, the king of Moab, who sent for him. The verse adds that the Lord's anger was kindled against Balaam because of this, and that the angel of Yahweh took his stand in the road as an adversary.[36] Balaam was riding on his ass and his two servants accompanied him. The ass saw the angel of Yahweh standing in the road with a drawn sword in his hand, and the ass turned aside out of the road and went into a field. Balaam's response was to strike the ass so as to turn her back onto the road (22:23).

Then the angel of Yahweh stood in a narrow path between the vineyards, with a wall on either side (22:24). But the ass saw the messenger of Yahweh and pushed against the wall to avoid him. In so doing, she inadvertently pressed Balaam's foot against the wall; Balaam's response was to strike the ass a second time (22:25). The purpose of the first blow was, explicitly, to turn the ass back onto the road; since no purpose is mentioned for the second, was it to punish the ass? This question arises as a consequence of what happens next.

The angel of the Lord then went ahead, and this time he stood in a place so narrow that there was no way to turn either to the right or to the left to avoid him (22:26). This time, when the ass saw the messenger of Yahweh and the impossibility of avoiding him by veering either to the right or to the left, she lay down under Balaam. The narrator comments that this time Balaam's anger was kindled against the ass. The same phrase is used here of Balaam as was used in verse 22 of God: his anger was kindled. God became angry because Balaam was going to Balak; now Balaam has become angry because the ass is veering from the way and preventing Balaam from going to Balak. Here the text is explicit: Balaam's anger was kindled, and as a consequence he struck the ass a third time (22:27).

The audience knows what Balaam doesn't know, that the ass has seen the messenger of Yahweh, who had been sent as an adversary against Balaam because of the Lord's anger. The audience knows also that the ass is acting as she is in order to avoid the drawn sword of the angel of Yahweh.

At this point in the narrative the ass speaks. The text says explicitly that the Lord opened the mouth of the ass. The Lord enables the ass to perform an activity usually associated with human beings. The ass asks Balaam, "What have I done to you, that you have struck me these three times?" (22:28).

The ass's words are spoken neither in anger for the treatment she has received nor in self-defense. The ass does not explain, "I've been protecting you from the drawn sword of the angel of Yahweh." Rather, she asks a question, assuming the posture of one who honestly doesn't know, who admits her ignorance in the hope that she will be brought to understanding. Balaam replies, "Because you have made a fool of me."[37]

The audience knows just how far off the mark Balaam is. The ass has not been making sport of Balaam; she has been protecting him from the drawn sword of the angel of Yahweh. Balaam's anger seems to be caused by his perception that she has behaved as she willed rather than as he willed, that she has acted with self-initiative rather than with obedience and conformity. Balaam seems to have concluded that the ass has dared to upset the power relations between them. By not going directly along the road, the way that Balaam had set, the ass was humiliating him, daring to challenge the hierarchical relationship Balaam assumed between himself and the animal. Whereas Balak had offered Balaam "honor" (22:17) if he would go to him and curse Israel (see 22:37), Balaam seems to conclude from the ass's behavior that she is dishonoring him.

Balaam goes on to say to the ass, "I wish I had a sword in my hand, for then I would kill you" (22:29). The audience appreciates the irony of Balaam's words. It is the angel of Yahweh who has a drawn sword in his hand, and who would have killed Balaam but for the loyal and courageous protection of the ass. Balaam is not justified in his anger toward the ass; the ass, on the other hand, might be justly angry because of Balaam's behavior toward her.

Despite Balaam's reply to her question, the ass continues the conversation by appealing to her long-standing relationship with Balaam. Her questions are deeply penetrating, personal, and relational: "Am I not your ass on which you have ridden all your life long until this day? Was I ever accustomed to do so to you?" (22:30).

Whereas Balaam has presumed hierarchy and the legitimation of domination, presumptions out of which he deliberately struck his ass three times, the ass appeals not to hierarchy but to interdependence, to a long relationship between the two beings, a relationship that has endured during Balaam's whole life, a relationship in which the ass has always acted faithfully, that is, in Balaam's best interests. The ass's third question forces Balaam to reflect on the past and to admit that the ass has never acted in such a manner toward him before now.

At this point what does Balaam know? He knows his ass has behaved strangely. Maybe he knows that he shouldn't have acted so quickly to strike her. Maybe he even recognizes that he doesn't know why his ass has behaved as she did; that is, maybe he even knows that he doesn't have all the answers. Would Balaam have spoken again to the ass, this time, for the first time, himself asking a question? Would he have put himself in a position of admitting that the ass had, at least in this situation, superior knowledge? Would he have been humble enough to acknowledge the ass's superior knowledge by asking the ass why she behaved as she did? Balaam never asks.

The narrator breaks in. Just as the Lord had opened the ass's mouth, the narrator reports that the Lord now opened Balaam's eyes (22:31). Balaam could now see what the ass had seen all along: the messenger of Yahweh standing in the way, holding his drawn sword (22:31). Whereas Balaam's response to the ass had been to presume and to strike her, Balaam's response to the angel is one of submission. He bows his head and falls on his face (22:31).

Balaam behaves very differently toward one he understands to be his superior than he does toward a mere animal. A dialogue now follows between the messenger of Yahweh and Balaam, another dialogue that begins with a question. The angel does not commence by explaining to Balaam the cause of the Lord's anger and his consequent drawn sword.

Rather, he puts himself in the position of the petitioner, asking Balaam to explain what he, the messenger, does not understand. Taking up the cause of the ass, the messenger of Yahweh asks Balaam, "Why have you struck your ass these three times?" (22:32). Before Balaam has a chance to answer, the messenger of Yahweh continues. As if circumstantially, he says, "I have come forth to withstand you, because your way is perverse before me" (22:32). Though the Hebrew here translated "perverse" is unclear and the text is therefore open to interpretation, the phrase is generally translated so that it reinforces the role of the messenger of Yahweh as Balaam's adversary (compare 22:22). The messenger of Yahweh had become Balaam's adversary because Balaam was going to Balak and God's anger was therefore kindled against him. Now this assertion by the messenger of his relationship to Balaam is sandwiched between a question and a statement about the ass. Is Balaam's treatment of his ass another example of the perversity of Balaam's behavior?

In defense of the ass, the messenger of Yahweh says, "The ass saw me and turned aside before me these three times. If she had not turned aside from me, surely just now I would have slain you and let her live" (22:33). Because the ass had seen the messenger of the Lord and responded protectively, her life would have been spared; because Balaam had acted contrary to the will of God, the angel of the Lord, sent as an adversary to Balaam, would have killed him.

Balaam's response is not to the ass but to the messenger. He acknowledges that he has sinned, that he didn't know that the angel stood in the road against him, and that if going to Balak is evil, he will return home (22:34). Balaam never admits explicitly to wronging the ass; any admission of wrongdoing toward the ass is subsumed in what is either a more general admission of sin or an admission that going to Balak against the will of God is wrong.

The angel's response to Balaam is the following: "Go with the men; but only the word which I bid you, that shall you speak" (22:35). There is irony even in this final directive. The ass had spoken only after the Lord had opened her mouth; Balaam was now charged, not to be superior to the ass as he had presumed he was, but to be like the ass. Just as God has opened the ass's mouth, so God would open Balaam's. Balaam, contrary to his superior sense of self, is here directed by one whom he considers his superior to become like the ass.

Summary and Conclusions

This chapter touches merely the tip of the iceberg. In the twentieth century, but especially in the last thirty years, the daughters of Sarah have experienced the influence of feminism on Christianity and the influence of Christian feminists on scriptural and theological interpretation. Scriptural texts, traditional interpretations of texts, and traditional doctrinal formulations have been subjected to careful scrutiny and criticized for their patriarchal and hierarchical biases.

But such deconstructing is only part of the project. Attempts also have been made to preserve and to celebrate that part of the tradition that is salvageable and salvific. As a consequence, new paradigms for theological and scriptural interpretation have been and are continuing to be developed.

This chapter has first tried to highlight the relationship of ordination and the theological education of women in the latter part of the twentieth century. With very broad strokes it has tried to trace women's participation in uncovering the patriarchal biases of the biblical texts and their patriarchal interpretations, as well as women's participation in the reconstruction of biblical interpretation and theological formulations. Finally, the chapter has offered two examples of close readings of biblical texts, one from a feminist perspective and the other from an ecofeminist perspective. Though they are only examples, they are simple enough, I hope, to provide those not familiar with the efforts of Christian feminists with an introduction to their possibilities.

As diverse as Christian feminists are, most are committed to working toward a future whose theological reflection will include participation and leadership by women, by minorities, and by society's oppressed of whatever sort; they are committed to working toward a future in which power can be shared, and in which hierarchical relationships can be replaced by relationships of reciprocity and mutuality grounded in a profound respect for human and cosmic interdependence.

Notes

1. See Barbara Brown Zikmund, "Women and Ordination," in *In Our Own Voices: Four Centuries of American Women's Religious Writing*, ed. Rosemary Radford Ruether and Rosemary Skinner Keller (San Francisco: Harper, 1995), 293–310. According to Zikmund, the Holiness and Pentecostal denominations ordained women in great numbers around the end of the nineteenth century but the practice declined after 1920. Still, over 50 percent of the ordained women have consistently served in the Pentecostal, evangelical, and paramilitary denominations (p. 299). She cites Constance H. Jacquet, Jr., for the finding that in 1977 only 17 percent of women clergy were found in the ten major Protestant denominations (*Women Ministers in 1977* [New York: National Council of Churches, 1978], 7).

2. Daly, *Beyond God the Father* (Boston: Beacon Press, 1973), and *The Church and the Second Sex* (Boston: Beacon Press, 1985).

3. In other words, they employ a "hermeneutics of suspicion."

4. New York: Simon and Schuster, 1974.

5. New York: Seabury Press, 1975.

6. In other words, she employed a "liberation hermeneutics."

7. San Francisco: Harper and Row, 1988. The volume incorporates a "hermeneutics of imagination."

8. Rosemary Ruether, ed., *Gaia and God* (San Francisco: Harper, 1992).

9. By 1991, there was a sufficient number of publishing Christian feminists that Shelley Davis Finson was able to produce *Women and Religion: A Bibliographic Guide to Christian Feminist Liberation Theology* (Toronto: University of Toronto Press, 1991).

10. Philadelphia: Fortress, 1978. Trible, for example, retells the story of Genesis 2–3 as "A Love Story Gone Awry," in counterpoint to her interpretation of the Song of Songs as "Love's Lyrics Redeemed."

11. Philadelphia: Fortress, 1984. Trible tells the story of Hagar (Gen. 16:1–16, 21:9–21) as "The Desolation of Rejection"; of Tamar's rape (2 Sam. 13:1–22) as "The Royal Rage of Wisdom"; of Jephthah's daughter (Judg. 11:19–40) as "An Inhuman Sacrifice"; and of the unnamed women in Judg. 19:1–30 as "The Extravagance of Violence."

12. Louisville, Ky.: Westminster/John Knox Press, 1994.

13. New York: Crossroad, 1983.

14. Boston: Beacon Press, 1984.

15. (Boston: Beacon Press, 1992). See also Fiorenza's *Discipleship of Equals: A Critical Feminist ekklesialogy of Liberation* (New York: Crossroad, 1993), and *Jesus, Miriam's Child, Sophia's Prophet: Critical Issues in Feminist Christology* (New York: Continuum, 1994).

16. At the present time there is no comprehensive bibliographic guide to Christian feminist biblical interpretation nor is it possible to compile one here. Nevertheless, acknowledgment must be made of the ever-increasing number of biblical scholars who currently work from a feminist perspective.

17. (Louisville, Ky.: Westminster/John Knox Press, 1992).

18. *Searching the Scriptures: A Feminist Commentary,* 2 vols. (New York: Crossroad, 1994).

19. Only by way of example, one notes that Larry Boadt's *Reading the Old Testament: An Introduction* devotes an entire chapter to patriarchy and its effect in the social life of the people of ancient Israel. Francis Frick's *A Journey through the Hebrew Scriptures* replaces the traditional title "The Era of the Patriarchs" with "The Era of the Patriarchs and Matriarchs" and alters a traditional treatment of Genesis 12–50 accordingly.

20. See especially the New Revised Standard Version, which has multiple editions.

21. The interpretation presented here is an adaptation of one section of a paper I delivered at the Catholic Biblical Association's annual meeting in San Fran-

cisco, August 14, 1985. See also my *Introduction to the Old Testament: A Feminist Perspective* (Philadelphia: Fortress Press, 1988), 213–17.

Perhaps Vashti has remained in the shadows because she and the story are fiction, or because the situation that leads to Vashti's expulsion from her role as queen is believed to be merely a literary device to explain why the Jewess Esther could come to the throne and to thus facilitate the development of the central theme of the narrative. The Book of Esther has often been understood as being about neither Vashti nor even Esther; rather it is thought to function as a literary justification for the feast of Purim.

22. Seven is frequently used in the biblical texts as a symbolic number for completion. It is for this reason that questions regarding the possibility of only one banquet and the uncertainty of its duration emerged.

23. Twice elsewhere in the Old Testament when the hearts of men are merry, someone is victimized. In Judges 16:25 it is when the Philistines' hearts are merry that they wish to bring Samson on the scene that he might make sport for them; in 2 Sam. 13:28, Absalom orders his servants to wait until his brother Amnon's heart is merry with wine before killing him.

24. Wine drinking occurs at least three other times in the book of Esther. Twice Ahasuerus, drinking wine at Esther's dinners, is "most disposed to grant the queen's request" (5:6, 7:2); once, when Haman, in the place where they had been drinking wine, appeals to Esther to intercede for him to the king, Ahasuerus enters and, seeing Haman's posture, concludes that he is attacking the queen, violating harem prohibitions and his possession (7:8).

25. Throughout this reading and the reading of Num. 22:21–35 that follows, the New Revised Standard Version of the Bible has been quoted unless otherwise indicated.

26. The text presents eunuchs and wise men as having ready access to the king while communication between wife and husband takes place through intermediaries.

27. Consider that drinking, which got Ahasuerus into this predicament in the first place, was done according to the law (1:8).

28. Reading *timreynāh* rather than *tō'marnāh*, using the Stuttgart emendation.

29. Apparently there was no law to cover this situation. Was this because, as many commentators suggest, the incident was trivial, or because few women in that patriarchal society rebelled against their husbands? Was it because few refused to be men's possessions and sex objects, and those who did were themselves not in positions of influence and were easily quelled?

30. In contrast to the narrative's repetition of the number seven (seven days for the feast, seven eunuchs, seven wise men), its repetition of the wide repercussions of Vashti's act (all the peoples, all the princes, all the provinces, all women will hear of it), its repetition of the extent to which the king's decree was promulgated (to all provinces, every province, every people, every man), its threefold repetition of the fact that the king's message was conveyed to the queen by the

eunuchs, and its repeated plays on the phrase "before the king"—in contrast to all this, there is no precise repetition of or emphasis on Memucan's suggestion to displace Vashti. One can only speculate about the disparity: was it to achieve dramatic effect by contrast? to indicate that Memucan's first effort succeeded in reinforcing the docility of all women? to emphasize the other details and suggest a weaker status for the edict?

31. The denominative verb śārar, used here in its *qal* participial form, is very rare; it occurs only four times in the entire Old Testament and never elsewhere to describe the relationship between husband and wife.

32. The hierarchical relationship of husband to wife is more frequently expressed by the Hebrew bā'al.

33. See also Neh. 13:23–24.

34. The interpretation presented here is part of a longer paper presented at the annual meeting of the Catholic Biblical Association in Atchison, Kansas, August 15, 1993. See also my *Appreciating God's Creation through Scripture* (New York: Paulist Press, 1997), 37–42, for a popular reading of this text. Note the decentering of Balaam and the reclaiming of the ass. Acknowledging our current social location, in a precariously balanced ecosystem, I deliberately approached the interpretation of this text from a non-anthropocentric perspective. Consciousness of cosmic interdependence and the incorporation of the reality of interdependence among plants, animals, the elements, and humans is essential to ecofeminist biblical interpretation.

The only other animal in the Old Testament that speaks is the serpent (Gen. 3:1, 3:4–5).

35. The Hebrew word here translated ass, 'ātōn, is feminine.

36. The Hebrew word mal'āk may be translated either "messenger" or "angel" and often, as here, refers to one sent from God. The word is best translated "messenger" when he is visible and "angel" when he is not visible. Translation in this passage is difficult because the mal'āk is visible to the ass but only at the end of the passage is he visible to Balaam.

37. The Hebrew form of the verb used here, 'ālal, meaning "to play" or "to laugh," is here translated "make a fool of." In seven of the eight occurrences of the verb in the Hebrew Bible, the text has to do with unequal power relations, where one party is the victor and the other is the victim. In both 1 Sam. 31:4 and 1 Chron. 10:4, Saul pleads with his armor-bearer to kill him, lest the uncircumcised Philistines come and kill him and then "make sport of him." In Judg. 19:25 the men of the city "abused" the Levite's concubine. Jeremiah fears lest he be handed over to the Jews who had deserted to the Chaldeans and they "would abuse" him (Jer. 38:19). And in both Exod. 10:2 and 1 Sam. 6:6, reference is made to the God of Israel "making fools of" the Egyptians with plagues. See also Ps. 141:4.

4

Christian Feminist Theology

History and Future

ROSEMARY RADFORD RUETHER

What is Christian feminist theology and why do we need to do it? Basically, we need to do feminist theology as a corrective to a theology distorted by patriarchy, and in order to create a holistic theology that would not only include women as full members of the human and Christian community in their own right, but that would liberate women and men from sexist ideology and practice.

In theory, the task of theology in the Christian tradition should be the same for a woman as for a man. However, in practice, at this time in the history of Christianity, one must speak of a specific task and vocation for feminist theology in the Church. This is because, for most of its two-thousand-year history, the Christian Church has not only kept women from the ordained ministry but also from the study of theology and from the public roles of theologian and preacher.

In fact, proscriptions against women teaching publicly in the Church arose earlier and continue to be more stringent than bans against ordination. Perhaps this was because ordination was thought to be out of the question, while the possibility that the religious and intellectual gifts of women might afford them the status of teachers was continually seen as a threat to be averted. Already in the post-Pauline strata of the New Testament we find the forbidding of women as teachers in the Church: "I do not permit a woman to teach or to have authority over a man; she is to keep silence" (1 Tim. 2:12).

This early ban against women teachers reflects the fact that the earliest model of Christian leadership was drawn from the rabbinic role of teacher and also the likelihood that women were indeed engaged in teaching and public prophecy in the earliest Church. The ban against women teachers was repeated in third-century Church orders and reiterated in the Middle Ages and again in the Reformation in mainline Protestant traditions. Even in mid-nineteenth-century America, the Pauline dictum was used to object to women abolitionists who spoke in public assemblies.[1]

Christian theology was shaped in the patriarchal cultures and social realities of the Hebrew and Greco-Roman worlds and their medieval and modern Western heirs. This means that women were largely absent from the shaping of official Christian teaching, from its definitions of theology, spirituality, and sexuality, and the Church. Insofar as some women did participate in these arenas as contemplatives, teachers, and local leaders, their influence was seldom acknowledged; and when recognized, it was edited to make it acceptable to the patriarchal leadership. Women, half the human race, with their distinct psycho-physical and social experiences, have not been able to enter into conversation about God and humans, good and evil, truth and falsehood, sin and salvation, from their own vantage point.

Women were not only silenced and excluded from the shaping of the Christian tradition, but this tradition has been largely biased against them, through the need to justify and reinforce their silence and absence. The justification of women's exclusion has taken the form of endlessly reiterated dictates that define women as irrational and morally inferior expressions of the human species, or else idealized and sentimentalized beings whose essence is maternity, and in either case unfit by their very nature to teach or minister. Elite or dominant males and their experience were assumed to be normative for humanity as such. When women are noticed at all, it is only to define them as the "other," confined to limited roles and excluded from public leadership in church and society.

This exclusion of women and its justifications result in a systematic distortion of all the symbols of Christian theology by patriarchal bias. The imagery and understanding of God, Christ, human nature, sin, salvation, church, and ministry were all shaped by a male-centered, misogynist worldview that subordinated women and rendered them non-normative and invisible. This must be seen not simply in the words or images for God, Christ, humanity, and ministry but also in the patterns assumed in the power relationships between all the key theological symbols.[2]

For example, God is not only imaged almost exclusively in male terms but also in terms of patriarchal power roles, such as patriarchal father, king, warrior, and lord. The relationship between God and humans is assumed to be one of omniscience, omnipotence, and absolute goodness and purity, over against humans who are weak, fallible, sinful, and impure. Spirituality or conversion has been classically conceived as a bottoming-out experience in which sinful humans recognize their utter worthlessness and submit totally to an all-powerful and all-good God as their only hope. Even this submission is seen as an arbitrary gift of a God who elects whom he chooses, since, in the Augustinian tradition, the dominant tradition of Western spirituality, it is believed that humans are so totally alienated from God that they are not even able to make the first act of repentence "on their own."[3]

Thus the relation between God and humans is seen as one of adversarial power, a zero-sum game of absolute power and goodness against worthlessness and powerlessness to choose the good. The relation is one of domination and submission absolutized. This view of God and relation to God reinforces the subjugation and denigration of women, since human nature considered in terms of sin, impurity, and weakness is identified particularly with women. Although men share these bad human tendencies, it is women who are seen both as epitomizing them and as being the original cause of the "fall of man" into sin.

In the sin-redemption relation to God in Christ, the male is seen as being transformed, caught up in a new humanity identified with Christ and able to represent Christ or God in the Church, while women remain only the objects, but never the agents, of redemption, at least officially. They receive redeeming grace, but they cannot be its official sacramental agents or exemplars. They are to be redeemed precisely by redoubling their acknowledgment of their unworthiness and their submission to God and God's agents, who are the male leaders in the Church, the family, and society.

The classical Catholic Christian insistence on the ontological necessity of the maleness of Christ epitomizes the patriarchal bias of the theological system. Christ must be male because, in some sense, God as both Father and Son is male, and so only a human male can represent God. The scholastic use of the Aristotelian tradition also defined the male as the one who possesses full and normative human nature, while women are defective and lack a humanity capable of representing the normatively human as such.[4]

The masculine distortion of God and Christ, human nature, sin, and salvation also biases the view of Church and ministry. Early Church Fathers, such as Saint Augustine, spoke of the Church as the virginal Mother who rescues us at baptism from our sinful origins in sexual procreation and birth by our fleshly mothers. The Church undoes the sin of Eve, represented by all women but particularly by sexually active women. Only males can represent God and Christ in the sacramental priesthood, channeling the grace won by Christ to overcome sin. The clergy-lay relation is represented as dominant all-knowing sacral males who administer saving grace to a fallen, female-identified laity. This construct reinforces the patriarchal gender relations of the family and society. Other hierarchical relations—lords to servants, parents to children, teachers to students, professionals to clients, ruling class to working class, dominant race to subjugated race—have also been reinforced through this basic hierarchical model of God to human, clergy to laity.

Feminist theology is a systematic critique of this patriarchal bias as it pervades the theological symbol system, both overtly in explicitly misogynist statements about female inferiority and culpability, and covertly in a pervasive androcentrism that makes the male the normative human in a way that renders the female invisible. Feminist theologians —particularly in the last thirty years, as women gained some access to formal theological education—have been unpacking this bias, both across the whole system of theological symbols and across the historical development of these symbols. They wish to make clear that this distortion is both broad and deep. It cannot be solved by a little linguistic tinkering. The whole symbolic system must be reconstructed, re-envisioned in all its parts and interrelations and in their implications for the practice of ministry in the Church.

Feminist theology moves through a three-stage dialectic, not simply as a linear process but as a continually deepening spiral of critique and reconstruction. The first stage consists of naming the problem. The patterns of androcentrism and misogyny in the tradition are recognized, analyzed, and delegitimated.[5]

The second stage takes the form of a quest for an alternative tradition in the scriptures and history of theology. Is androcentrism and misogyny the whole story? Is there no basis within the tradition itself for delegitimating the male bias? If there is not, perhaps Christianity is simply not capable of reform, and perhaps women and men concerned for liberation from patriarchy should leave Christianity and join or form some religious, social, and spiritual community that does recognize sexism as an evil from which we should be liberated. Several important feminist theologians, such as Mary Daly and Carol Christ, who began as Christians, have come to this conclusion and have left Christianity accordingly.[6]

Christian feminism, by contrast, regards sexism and patriarchy as deep-seated but not normative patterns in the Bible and the Christian tradition. Christian feminists believe that there are true resources in Biblical revelation, in Christ, and in the good news that flows from Christ, that not only do not validate sexism but undergird our struggle against it and liberation from it. Thus Christian feminist theology conducts its quest for alternative traditions to demonstrate this hypothesis and to make explicit the alternative traditions that stand against patriarchal distortion and point toward a new humanity and an earth liberated from patriarchy.[7]

The third stage of feminist theology, then, is concerned with reconstructing all the basic symbols of Christian faith to be equally inclusive of both women and men, and to lead toward liberatory faith and practice. What would it mean to reconstruct Christian theology from its androcentric, misogynist forms to egalitarian, liberating inclusiveness and mutuality? This implies a clear rejection of the lingering assumption that patriarchy is the divinely ordained order of creation and of the Church. It means naming patriarchy as sin, as unjust, as a distorted relationality that corrupts the humanity of both men and women. It also means a rejection of any gynecentric reversal of gender relations and symbols that makes women the primary exemplars of true humanity and the divine image, and regards men as defective humans, essentially prone to evil in ways that women are not.[8]

Such an anthropology affirms that both women and men possess the fullness of human nature in all its complexity. They are not to relate to each other as superior to inferior or as complementary parts of a human nature in which each has what the other lacks. Rather—woman as woman, and man as man—each possesses the fullness of human potential. Their relation should be one of mutually transforming friendship that nurtures and enables the full and equivalent flowering of the human personhood of each in relation to others.

Feminist theology and spirituality name sexism as sin and patriarchy as a sinful social system. Sexism and patriarchy express sin as distortion of human relationality into domination and subjugation, corrupting the humanity of both men and women. Grace and conversion, the spiritual journey to liberation, then, is seen as beginning with the gift of critical consciousness to recognize and name such distortions as sinful, as illegitimate, to be converted from them and to struggle against them to overcome patriarchy, both in personal relationships and in social systems.

Redemption means building new relationships, personally and socially, that incarnate mutual co-humanity. God and Christ, far from incarnating patriarchal relationships, are the source of liberating grace to free us from such relationships and to ground and sustain our growth into mutual co-humanity.

The experience of Christ as the presence of God in our lives reveals the nature of God as the power of co-humanity. Christ is our revealed paradigm of the Logos-Sophia (Word-Wisdom) of God.[9] God's Word or Wisdom is both beyond male and female and yet can be personified in both women and men. The maleness of the human, historical person of Jesus of Nazareth in no way limits God or the incarnation of God to one gender. Rather Jesus' male gender is simply one expression of his particularity as a historical individual, just as his Jewishness was and the fact that he was born in a particular time and place and had particular physical features.

Jesus as a particular paradigmatic person is representative of God and authentic humanity precisely by pointing toward the true potential of all humans in all times and places, of all races and gender identities. In the ongoing community of faith we are called to encounter Jesus as the Christ, as that liberating potential of all humans, not limited by gender, race, social class, culture, time, or place. As a community called to witness against evil, we encounter Christ particularly in our sisters and brothers who are victims of injustice and who struggle against injustice, modeling transforming love.

A feminist view of ministry should begin with an understanding of Church as both a nurturing and a prophetic community of liberation from evil, including evil as patriarchy. As Church we seek to enter into just and loving co-humanity. Ministry should be the enabling of the community of faith to develop its life together as mutual birthing of our full humanity and as witness to the world of this people's exodus from patriarchy and its entrance into co-humanity in Christ.

This vision of an inclusive and liberating Christian community is not new. Feminists would see its roots in the original Jesus movement and early Church as a countercultural prophetic movement. But the patriarchalization of Christianity in the late first and second centuries obscured this vision within what became the canonical New Testament and marginalized it in the history of the Church.[10] Nevertheless the basic outlines of this understanding of Christianity were sufficiently evident in the New Testament that prophetic renewal movements have continually rediscovered it. Groups such as the Waldensians in the twelfth century and Quakers in the seventeenth century have glimpsed this vision and opened their ministry to women.[11]

Although it is possible today to trace a continual line of movements that have renewed this vision of the Gospel, it was not until women gained access to theological schools as students and then as teachers, as well as to the ordained ministry, that it has been possible to recreate its history, as well as to develop it more fully in the contemporary democratic cultural context. Although some women were ordained in Protestant churches in the period of the 1850s to the 1880s, the real breakthrough to women's ordination in mainline Protestantism did not begin until the late 1950s, and the increase of women in theological schools followed in the 1960s. Today the student bodies of theological schools of denominations that ordain women are 40 to 50 percent female, while anywhere from one or two to half of their faculty is female. Scholarship on women in the Bible, church history, and theology, as well as the other fields of theological education, has burgeoned in the last twenty-five years so that titles of major books and articles would easily fill a thousand pages, just in English.[12]

Feminist theology, however, is not confined to the North American or English-speaking worlds. In recent years, networks of Western European women have developed a pan-European society for theological research, as well as many national and local groups.[13] Several religious studies faculties in British universities have developed specialties on women's issues, and feminist theology has become a requirement in Dutch theological schools, both Protestant and Catholic. There is less openness to feminist perspectives in university-based theological faculties in Germany, and feminism is virtually excluded from church-controlled theological study in France and Italy, but European women are finding alternative educational programs in which to teach and study feminist theology. In Gelnhausen near Frankfurt, a lively group of feminist theologians and pastors do grassroots training in feminist theology, liturgy, and Bible drama.[14]

Feminist theology is also developing in Latin America. The Methodist University in São Paulo, Brazil, has a major research center on women's issues, while the Methodist-sponsored Comunidad Bíblica Teológica in Lima, Peru, has a Mesa de la Mujer that studies topics of feminist theology and women in Latin American church history. The

Lutheran theological faculty in São Leopoldo, Brazil, requires all students to take a course in feminist theology. The Universidad Bíblica in Costa Rica also offers feminist theology and is the base for a network of feminist pastors and theologians throughout Latin America and the Caribbean.[15]

Asians are also developing study centers, networks of women theologians who meet regularly, and journals for the publication of their writings. Asian women founded the journal *In God's Image* in 1982 as a vehicle for Asian women's theology. Its contributing board spans Asia from India, Sri Lanka, and Thailand, to China, Japan, Korea, and the Philippines. Often particular issues focus on one or another Asian country. The Asian Women's Resource Center located in Kuala Lumpur, Malaysia, organizes regular dialogues of Asian feminist theologians and publishes their reflections.[16] For example, in December 1990, delegations from seven Asian countries met for a week in Madras, India, to share papers on hermeneutical principles for feminist theology in each Asian context.

Africans have the fewest resources for such feminist reflection, but feminist theological programs are developing at some universities, such as the University of the Western Cape in South Africa. The Circle of Concerned African Women Theologians is the major network for periodic encounters and publications by African Christian feminists.[17] Even some Christian women in the Middle East, particularly Palestinians, are doing reflection on women's issues in the context of Palestinian liberation and contextual theologies.[18]

Since 1983 the major forum for Third World feminist theology has been the Women's Commission of the Ecumenical Association of Third World Theologians (EATWOT). This organization was founded in the 1970s to network liberation theologians from Latin America, Asia, and Africa. Few women delegates attended their early meetings, and women's issues were completely ignored. But by the end of the 1970s some women theologians, such as Mercy Oduyoye of Kenya, Sun Ai Park from Korea, Virginia Fabella from the Philippines, Ivone Gebara from Brazil, and Elza Tamez from Mexico, began to raise the issue of women in liberation theology. Mercy Oduyoye called the women's issue the "irruption within the irruption," the challenge that would require liberation theologians to rethink their theology, just as liberation theology has challenged traditional Christian theology.[19]

There was much resistance to feminist issues among the male liberation theologians of EATWOT. It was argued that feminism was a "First World issue," that it was a diversion from the "class struggle," and that it was alien to Third World cultures. But the women of EATWOT persisted, declaring that "it is not for First World women to define what feminism is for us, and also it is not for Third World men to say it is not our issue. We will define what feminism is for us." The EATWOT women called for a Women's Commission as a vehicle for the development of feminist theology in its various Third World contexts. As Mercy Amba Oduyoye and Virginia Fabella put it in the book that emerged from the major international gathering of this network,

> We, the women of the Association, were just as concerned to name the demons and to have them exorcised. Sexism was one such demon, and it existed within the Association itself. Our voices were not being heard, although we were visible enough. It became clear to us that only the oppressed can truly name their oppression. We demanded to be heard. The result was the creation within EATWOT of a Women's Commission, and not a Commission on Women, as some of the male members would have it. Rather than see ourselves solely as victims of male domination, we formed a sisterhood of resistance to all forms of oppression, seeking creative partnership with the men of the Association.[20]

Over the next five years, a series of assemblies on Third World feminist theology took place through the organizational initiatives of the Women's Commission. The assemblies were planned to take place in four stages. First there would be national meetings, then continental meetings, then a global meeting of the three regions of Asia, Africa, and Latin America. Finally there would be a fourth meeting in which Third World feminist theologians would meet with First World feminist theologians from Europe and North America. The first three stages of national and continental meetings and a Third World global meeting took place over the period 1983–1986. After these assemblies, the Third World women began deepening their global ties and developing journals and networks.

The long-planned Third–First World gathering took place in Costa Rica in December 1994. Here the Third World groups met in a new stage of dialogue with feminist theologians from Western Europe and North America. But it was recognized that the fall of the Communist states in Eastern Europe had changed the definition of "Third World." It was decided to expand the dialogue to include feminist theologians from Eastern Europe, the Middle East, and the Pacific.

The United Nations meetings in Cairo and in Beijing in September 1994 and 1995 brought fresh evidence that women's status worldwide is not improving. In many ways the growing global split between wealth and poverty, the proliferation of armed struggles and local lawlessness, and the deterioration of the environment have the greatest impact upon poor women and children. The gathering of First and Third World women theologians in Costa Rica made these many-sided aspects of violence against women the focus of their theological reflections.[21]

What are the distinctive issues of Third World Christian feminist theology? How do feminist thinkers from such diverse regions as Brazil and Mexico, India, Korea, the Philippines, Ghana, Nigeria, and South Africa contextualize feminist reflection in their ecclesial, social, cultural, and historical situations? Despite enormous differences in context, there are many similarities in the way Third World women construct a feminist critique on such major Christian doctrines as God language, Christology, Church, and ministry.

These similarities reflect the fact that these women are not only Christians but they received their Christianity, for the most part, from Western European and North American missionaries. In India, Christianity has been present since the second or third century, but even there the dominant Christian churches reflect the Catholic missions that began in the sixteenth century and the Protestant missions that arrived with British colonialism in the nineteenth century. Christianity came to the Philippines with the Spanish in the sixteenth century, and was reshaped by American Protestants from the end of the nineteenth century. Koreans also experienced earlier Catholic missionary efforts, but most of Korean Christianity today is the fruit of American Protestant missionary work from the late nineteenth century.

These predominantly colonial origins of Asian, African, and Latin American Christianity mean that the Christian women theologians of these regions have been educated in the Western European and North American Catholic or Protestant cultures imported to their regions. For some, even the languages in which they write were imposed by the European and American colonists: Spanish, Portuguese, English, and French. Their ancestors became Christians by being uprooted from their indigenous cultures and religions, which were represented to them by Western missionaries as inferior and idolatrous evils to be shunned.

Thus, Third World feminist theologians find themselves having to address theological problems imposed on them by Western missionaries, and also social injustices brought by the Western colonization that was the vehicle of Christianization. Third World women find common ground with each other in similar problems of socioeconomic and cultural colonialism and its contemporary expressions in neocolonial dependency and exploitation. The issues of sexism and patriarchy add another layer to these issues of cultural and social colonialism, often worsening (contrary to the claims of Christian missionaries), rather than alleviating, patterns of sexism found in the indigenous culture.

Women in Mexico, India, Korea, Nigeria, or South Africa find themselves with colonial and missionary versions of Christian male clericalism. They hear versions, often in the most authoritarian, fundamentalist tones, of the same biblical and theological arguments that declare that God has created male leadership and has forbidden women's ordained ministry in the Church. Thus, Third World feminist theologians find the writings of First World feminist biblical critics, such as Elisabeth S. Fiorenza, highly useful in addressing the issues of the patriarchal nature and use of the Bible, not as a "First World issue" but as an issue that has been exported into their context and that they have to confront in their own churches and theological schools.

In the Asian feminist hermeneutic papers from the 1990 Madras gathering, the authors define a double dialogue that situates their own contextualization of feminist theology. On one side, they acknowledge their debt to First World feminist theologians and theorists but also recognize the inadequacy of this work for them and their need to do their own contextualization of feminist critique. On the other side, they are in dialogue with the male liberation theologians of their countries. They regard their feminist work as part of the struggle for national liberation, deepening that struggle to include gender and the oppression of women.[22]

But Asian women must also deplore the fact that hardly any of their male liberation colleagues have been willing to incorporate this feminist reflection. This is not necessarily because of a determined hostility but rather an apparent inability to understand women's experience and to place gender oppression on a par with class oppression. Thus it becomes evident that feminist theology cannot wait for "permission" from male theologians. It must first be developed by women.

Third World feminist theology typically begins with storytelling from women's experience, and moves on to social analysis based on women's stories. The paper presented at Madras from the Filipino women begins with five first-person stories: Lucy, a factory worker; Norma, a college student and victim of incest; Elisa, a former political detainee tortured in prison; Lotia, a bar girl; and Sister Jannie, a religious sister from a tribal region. The paper uses these five stories to analyze Filipino women's social context. Their vulnerability to sexual abuse at home and on the job, their low wages, and the double exploitation of their labor in the family and in the paid economy are placed in a broad analytical framework.

The paper also shows how Christianity validated the cultural uprooting of the Filipino people and Filipino women's particular subjugation as women. But the paper also sees positive resources for women in the historical past—particularly in the reclaiming of indigenous Filipino spirituality, but also in the liberatory aspects of the biblical and Christian traditions and in the history of Filipino women's resistance to oppression.[23]

This analysis of women's subjugation consciously reaches beyond a middle-class feminism of equality to a liberation feminism. That is, it locates gender oppression, historically and socially, in relation to the history of class, race, and national oppression. It looks at women's situation within class hierarchy and in relation to both traditional culture and colonialism. Liberation theology's "preferential option for the poor" thus takes on a more concrete focus. It means particularly a solidarity with the most oppressed and exploited women of their societies, the poorest of the poor, or the *minjung* of the *minjung*, as Korean women put it.[24]

Third World women are also clear that exploitation and violence to women are not only an issue for poor women but rather cut across class lines. This is particularly true of domestic violence and sexual abuse. There is rape and incest of the female child in the home, and wife battering and denial of reproductive rights, even in affluent families. But these burdens are far greater for poor women.

While these patterns of women's oppression could be found in Western societies, Third World women also focus on aspects of women's suffering that are specific to their societies. For example, a major focus of feminist organizing in India has been the "dowry murders" or attempted murders. In India the dowry has become commercialized in recent years. It is not unusual for the groom's family to demand large sums of money and expensive consumer goods, such as stereo sets and motorcycles, as the price of taking a bride into the family. If the groom and his family are dissatisfied with these gifts, kitchen "accidents" have often been arranged to burn the hapless bride to death. The family then goes shopping for a second bride and dowry. Tens of thousands of Indian women have been killed or maimed in such assaults. The high price of dowries has also encouraged a widespread practice of female feticide. These realities had been ignored until Indian feminists gathered information and organized against them.[25]

A particularly sensitive issue for Third World Christian feminists in relation to the Christian churches has been religious pluralism. Christianity is the religion of a small minority in Asia, except in the Philippines and South Korea. Most Asians are Hindus, Buddhists, Confucianists, or they follow tribal forms of shamanism, often in combination. While Christianity is expanding in black Africa, the indigenous religions, as well as Islam, also persist. Even in Latin America there is a rediscovery of the indigenous forms of spirituality repressed for centuries by the Spanish conquerors.

Although Asian and African male liberation theologians claim a positive relation to the other religions of their communities, this issue has particular significance for women.[26] Third World feminists have questioned the ways in which male Christian theologians have appropriated aspects of indigenous culture and religion, seeing these appropriations as sometimes romantic and unhistorical but also as overlooking or justifying the oppressive aspects of these cultures for women.[27] Sometimes Christianity is even used to reinforce aspects of the traditional culture that confine women, such as Indian Christian pastors who enforce menstrual taboos from Hebrew scripture, perpetuating assumptions of women's ritual impurity found in Hindu caste traditions.[28]

At the same time, Third World feminists are also searching the indigenous heritage for positive recoverable traditions for women. Korean women reclaim elements of shamanism, while Filipino women discover useful tradition in precolonial Filipino myths and women priests. Indian women use the Hindu idea of Shakti, or the feminine cosmic power that underlies all life, as a positive motif, while the Andean women of Latin America explore the pre-Hispanic earth goddess Pachamama.

Third World Christian feminists also claim the liberating traditions of the Bible, despite the failure of the churches and even male liberation theologians to apply these to women. They are doing their own contextualization of biblical traditions to find usable elements for women's emancipation in their societies. They establish a relation to the religious cultures and social injustices of their societies that is complex and dialectical, refusing to repudiate their Western liberationist and Christian traditions in toto in the name of anticolonial liberation, but also refusing to reject their indigenous traditions in the name of biblical exclusivism. They wish to excise the patriarchal elements from both these cultures while bringing together the liberating elements of prophetic faith and holistic cosmologies in a new synthesis.

Today it is no exaggeration to say that Christian feminist theology is global. It seeks to bring together global consciousness with the rich particularity of each local culture. Feminists seek to position their theological reflection on God, Christ, and the Church, sin and salvation, in the context of world patterns of structural violence and injustice to women and to the poor, as well as the impoverishment of the earth itself by exploitative misuse.

Although Christian feminist theology is now both widespread and diverse, the struggle for acceptance of its critique is far from over. Male theologians, even liberation theologians, often ignore it or seek to delegitimize it. The struggle to incorporate feminist reflection in theological education and in preaching and worship in local churches has only begun. Feminist theologians know that the power of the patriarchal church establishment, which buttresses the dominant hierarchies in society, is formidable. But they also know that prophets have never been well received, including the one whom Christians call their Lord. For them, only a gospel that is really inclusive of women in all cultures and peoples deserves to be called "good news."

Notes

1. On the conflict between abolitionist preachers Sarah and Angelina Grimké and the Massachusetts Congregational clergy who objected to their lecturing in public because it violated "biblical norms" for women, see Larry Ceplair, *The Public Years of Sarah and Angelina Grimké: Selected Writing, 1835–1839* (New York: Columbia University Press, 1989), 135–299; also see Barbara Brown Zikmund, "The Struggle for the Right to Preach," in Rosemary R. Ruether and Rosemary S. Keller, eds., *Women and Religion in America: The Nineteenth Century* (San Francisco: Harper and Row, 1981), 193–240.

2. For a fuller exposition of the perspective of this essay, see Rosemary Radford Ruether, *Sexism and God-talk: Toward a Feminist Theology* (Boston: Beacon Press, 1983, 1993).

3 For the primary sources for Augustine's theological anthropology in his controversy with Pelagius, see J. Patout Burns, *Theological Anthropology* (Philadelphia: Fortress, 1981), 10–22, 39–108.

4. See the Vatican declaration against women's ordination and a critical commentary, ed. Leonard and Arlene Swidler, *Women Priests: A Catholic Commentary on the Vatican Declaration* (New York: Paulist Press, 1977).

5. See Mary Daly, *The Church and the Second Sex* (New York: Harper and Row, 1968); also Rosemary Radford Ruether, ed., *Religion and Sexism: Images of Women in the Jewish and Christian Traditions* (New York: Simon and Schuster, 1974).

6. See Mary Daly, *Beyond God the Father: Toward a Philosophy of Women's Liberation* (Boston: Beacon, 1973), and Carol Christ, *The Laughter of Aphrodite: Reflections on a Journey to the Goddess* (San Francisco: Harper and Row, 1987).

7. See Rosemary Radford Ruether and Eleanor McLaughlin, eds., *Women of Spirit: Female Leadership in the Jewish and Christian Traditions* (New York: Simon and Schuster, 1979).

8. For example, see Anne Carr, *Transforming Grace: Christian Tradition and Women's Experience* (San Francisco: Harper and Row, 1988); also Catherine M. LaCugna, ed., *Freeing Theology: The Essentials of Theology in Feminist Perspective* (San Francisco: Harper, 1993).

9. For an understanding of God developed from a Sophialogical perspective, see Elizabeth Johnson, *She Who Is: The Mystery of God in Feminist Theological Discourse* (New York: Crossroad, 1993).

10. See Elizabeth Schuessler Fiorenza, *In Memory of Her: A Feminist Theological Reconstruction of Christian Origins* (New York: Crossroad, 1983).

11. See Rosemary Radford Ruether, *Women Church: Theology and Practice* (San Francisco: Harper and Row, 1986).

12. For a bibliography up to 1990, see Shelley D. Finson, *Women and Religion: A Bibliographic Guide to Christian Feminist Liberation Theology* (Toronto: University of Toronto Press, 1991).

13. For feminist theological networks and teaching in Europe and the Third World, see Rosemary Radford Ruether, "Christianity and Women in the Modern World," in *Today's Women in World Religion*, ed. Arvind Sharma (Albany: SUNY Press, 1994), 267–302.

14. This group is the Frauenstudien und Bildungszentrum, located at Burchhardhaus, D-63571, Gelnhausen, Germany. Among its organizers are Herta Leistner and Ute Knie.

15. In June–July 1996, I spoke for these groups in Brazil and Peru; thus these remarks come from personal experience.

16. The Asian Women's Resource Center is located at 79 Lorong Anggor, Taman Shanghai, 58100 Kuala Lumpur, Malaysia.

17. See the book edited by Mercy Amba Oduyoye and Musimbi R. A. Kanyoro, *The Will to Arise: Women, Tradition and Church in Africa* (Maryknoll, N.Y.: Orbis, 1992).

18. The Palestinian women's theologial critique is very low-key and is contacted primarily through the Sabeel Palestinian Liberation Theology Center, connected with St. George's Cathedral in East Jerusalem. See Rosemary R. Ruether, Marc Ellis, and Naim Ateek, eds., *Faith and the Intifada: Palestinian Christian Voices* (Boston: Beacon Press, 1992), 119–32.

19. See Mercy Amba Oduyoye, "Reflections from a Third World Woman's Perspective," in *The Irruption of the Third World: Challenge to Theology,* ed. Virginia Fabella and Sergio Torres (Maryknoll, N.Y.: Orbis Books, 1983), 246–55.

20. Mercy Amba Oduyoye and Virginia Fabella, eds., *With Passion and Compassion: Third World Women Doing Theology* (Maryknoll, N.Y.: Orbis Books, 1988), ix–x.

21. For an account of this conference see my column in the *National Catholic Reporter,* January 27, 1995, p. 19. The papers from this conference have not been published.

22. These hermeneutical papers are being edited by the Asian Women's Resource Center but have not yet appeared. I have unpublished typescripts of the Filipino, Indian, Korean, and Hong Kong papers.

23. The Filipino paper was published separately as a pamphlet titled "Toward an Asian Principle of Interpretation: A Filipino Women's Experience," by the Women's Center at St. Scholastica College in Manila.

24. See Chung Hyun Khung, "Han Pu-ri: Doing Theology from Korean Women's Perspective," in *We Dare to Dream*, ed. Virginia Fabella and Sun Ai Park (Maryknoll, N.Y.: Orbis Books, 1989), 135–46; see also her *The Struggle to Be the Sun Again: Introducing Asian Women's Theology* (Maryknoll, N.Y.: Orbis Books, 1989).

25. On the campaign against dowry murders, see especially the Indian feminist magazine *Manuschi*, published in New Delhi.

26. The best-known African theologian who began the work of using African indigenous tradition is John Mbiti; see his *African Religions and Philosophy* (Garden City, N.Y.: Doubleday, 1970). The Sri Lankan Jesuit, Aloysius Pieris, has been a major figure for a Christian theology in dialogue with Buddhism; see his *An Asian Theology of Liberation* (Maryknoll, N.Y.: Orbis Books, 1988).

27. See Mercy Amba Oduyoye, *Daughters of Anowa: African Women and Patriarchy* (Maryknoll, N.Y.: Orbis Books, 1995).

28. This information on the imposition of menstrual taboos by Indian Protestant pastors on women members of their congregations, based on the revival of texts from the Levitical codes, came from discussions with women seminarians at the Gurukul Lutheran College in Madras, India, in January 1991.

5

Hagar

A Historical Model for "Gender Jihad"

HIBBA ABUGIDEIRI

Islamic scholars in search of scriptural exegesis or of modern revisionist interpretations of Hagar will be struck by the paucity of sources when compared with what may be found in the Judeo-Christian traditions. This is no accident. Indeed, the Islamic written tradition, whether scriptural or exegetical, speaks very little of Hagar because she simply does not carry the same exegetical significance in Islam that she does in its twin monotheistic predecessors. Her name nevertheless is penned in a few works by some prominent Muslim exegetes: Ibn Ishaq (d. 767), al-Tabari (d. 923), and Ibn Kathir (d. 1373), to name a few.[1] Her near absence from Islamic texts is not necessarily because of her sex; rather, it comes from the lack of dispute surrounding her significance in Islam.

For Muslims, Hagar is inarguably the mother of Abraham's oldest son, Isma'il. Her role in Islamic history that ultimately produced the Arab and later Muslim civilization speaks directly to the Muslim belief in Hagar's divine appointment. In short, there is no question of religious legitimacy involved in Hagar's hagiography in Islam, just as there is no question of that of Sarah. A participant in Abraham's mission to reestablish true monotheism on earth, Hagar is the ancestor of Abraham's heirs, the Muslims, since it was her descendant, Prophet Muhammad, who restored Abraham's religion after the world had once again fallen away from the true faith and proper worship of God.[2] Islamic exegetical literature has equally celebrated Sarah's motherhood for what it is: the continuation of the prophetic lineage to which most of the post-Abrahamic Qur'anic prophets and messengers belong.[3] Muslims, then, are simply not participants in the Sarah-Hagar legitimacy debate seen by some as integral to Judeo-Christian interfaith dialogue on the topic. Nor do they find it necessary to respond to the politicized discourse that ultimately sought to discredit Islam by appropriating Sarah as the sole legitimate matriarch.[4] To be the daughter of Hagar discards the Islamic lineage of Sarah. Muslim affinities extend to *both* matriarchs quite comfortably, and without contradiction.

Hagar's life, like that of other female figures of the Qur'an, provides moral lessons and real experiences relevant to contemporary Muslim women. In framing this chapter around the reexamined significance of Hagar within the Islamic tradition, I demonstrate how three modern Muslim women have come to serve as new models of Islamic leadership by using the same tool of empowerment that she did, namely, spiritual access to the divine. This chapter presents a brief discussion of how three American Muslim women have sustained, resisted, adjusted, or changed their historical roles as female leaders in light of the modern changes and challenges to Islam.[5] In discussing the contributions of Amina Wadud, Amira Sonbol, and Sharifa Alkhateeb, this study examines how contemporary Muslim women are renegotiating the very basis of Islamic leadership by adding an authoritative female voice. Despite the fact that the three work in different professional fields, the force of their contribution lies in the authority of a reinterpreted Qur'an that is used to reformulate new ideas about women, gender, and Muslim society, ideas that cannot easily be contested by the long-standing androcentric perspective of traditional Islam.[6]

This is not to suggest that the three women discussed here consciously pattern their lives and works around Hagar as a model of leadership. That would endow Hagar with greater archetypal power than she really holds among Muslim women. The point rather is that modern Muslim women, in their mission to establish God's will, draw from the same historical tool of reform used by Hagar to effect real change in society, namely, *taqwa*. Taqwa is not simply faith or God consciousness that molds these women into leaders. Rather, it is what their taqwa inspires them to accomplish. The real contribution of this study, then, is to highlight the historical continuity in the ways Muslim women draw power from their faith to correct the wrongs of society by being centered in God. In their attempt at social reform, modern women, like the Hagar of Islam's traditional past, reestablish female agency within a traditionally male Sunni orthodoxy.

This chapter could just as easily have focused on other female matriarchs of Islam, like Eve or Mary, in order to make its arguments about female access to God. Why Hagar? The figure of Hagar, as will be demonstrated, is a more appropriate figure through which new models of female Islamic leadership in the modern world can be critically reassessed. Her struggles and achievements provide striking parallels with the experiences of the women presented here. The allegorical narrative of Eve and the story of miraculous favor surrounding Mary do not offer a narrative of social liberation that Hagar's life history provides. Furthermore, there is a need to re-examine Hagar's significance, not in the context of interfaith dialogue but in terms of how her struggles as a woman seeking reform in a patriarchal society constitute a historically potent model of reform for modern Muslim women. Clearly, the figure of Hagar bridges traditionalism and modernity in ways that have not often been discussed in either Muslim circles or Islamic literature.

The Exegetical Hagar of Islam: Interpreted and Reinterpreted

The Qur'an never mentions Hagar by name in any of its 114 chapters, but reference is made to her in Abraham's prayer to God: "O my Lord! I have made *some of my offspring* [*dhuriyyati*] to dwell in a valley without cultivation, by the Sacred House, in order, O our Lord, that they may establish regular prayer. So fill the hearts of some among men with love towards them, and feed them with fruits so that they may give thanks" (14:37; emphasis added).

How Hagar has been historically conceived in the Muslim imagination is derived primarily from a few inauthenticated prophetic traditions (*ahadith*) as well as the Jewish and biblical traditions (*israiliyyat*) incorporated into the exegetical texts.[7] Hagar's hagiography is thus mainly constituted by, not Qur'anic revelation, but extra-Qur'anic tradition.[8] I use the israiliyyat here neither to contest variant Judeo-Christian scriptural interpretations of Hagar nor to test their Islamic validity. Rather, the ahadith and israiliyyat cited by Ibn Kathir and al-Bawwab that are used here proffer a glimpse of how Muslim religious thinkers historically viewed Hagar. Taking their interpretive view a step further, this chapter seeks to reinterpret the religious significance of Hagar in light of Muslim women's modern-day challenges and concerns. Thus, Hagar's near absence from scriptural commentary is not necessarily a signal of her insignificance; it may be quite the opposite. Hagar's absence may well signify a most formidable presence; it has only to be uncovered. What little that *is* said about the Egyptian slave speaks volumes when she is viewed on her own terms and not in relation to others. It is for this reason that I chose to analyze Hagar, not in relation to Abraham nor in opposition to Sarah, but as an independent historical example of a female reformer.

In short, Hagar constitutes an exemplary and powerful figure for demonstrating how female struggle and liberation remain integral aspects of Muslim women's modern lives, only now they are imbued with different meaning in response to contemporary issues. It is particularly during Hagar's trials of religious duty that her allegorical symbolism is most evident and best crystallized. Though many qualities about Hagar can be isolated for discussion, the one that is most outstanding and from which all others were derived is her taqwa. It was principally her God-consciousness that made her worthy of divine instruction, and that gave her the strength to persevere through her struggles to carve out an active female role within Islam.

Hagar: A Worthy Agent of God

Hagar's sacred history starts not with the birth of Isma'il. Although, like Mary, Hagar was given news of her divine mission by an angel after conception, it is crucial not to overstate the similarities between the two women. There are marked differences that are noteworthy: Mary was surrounded by miracles of divine favor since birth; she is the only female identified by name in the Qur'an (her name is also the title of a Qur'anic chapter); she was chosen and purified by God over all women of the worlds; and finally, she conceived miraculously.[9] Nevertheless, that Hagar received revelation in a manner similar to Mary not only confirms the unity of the Qur'an but also the worthiness of those to whom it was revealed. Both received an identical message—each would conceive a son whose name was revealed, and their sons were to become prophets of God, each with his own sacred mission.

Ibn Kathir reports that Hagar received her sacred assignment from God after conceiving Isma'il. Frightened by Sarah's jealousy, Hagar escaped into the woods, where an angel commanded her to return to Abraham's household. Assured that she would give birth to a male, and instructed to name him Isma'il—the one whom God would entrust to establish good and who would come to own the lands of his brothers—Hagar returned home to fulfill her sacred mission.[10] This divine instruction did not simply descend from the heavens upon Hagar, just as it did not fall randomly upon Mary. Both were chosen agents. That is, they had proven themselves worthy of divine instruction because of their God consciousness.

That Hagar was of slave origins had absolutely no bearing on her worthiness for divine appointment. In his *Tafsir al-Kabir,* al-Razi relates a dispute between Muslim religious scholars over the origin of Hagar's name.[11] One group viewed her name as stemming from the migration (*hijrah*) she made from Egypt to the Arabian Peninsula as part of her divine mission.[12] If such were the case, however, she would have been named the female migrator (*muhajirah*). The other, more plausible view argues that Hagar was so named because of her inclination to distance herself from evil (from the verb *hajara*, to dissociate oneself from profanity or evil), as the few practicing monotheists (*hunafah*) did in those days. In both cases, the Arabic root (*h-j-r*) of *both* designated names for Hagar is not accidentally identical. Both sides viewed Hagar, like Abraham, as a God-conscious monotheist (*hanifah*), a rarity in a pagan society. In fact, like Prophet Muhammad's adopted son Bilal, who was also of slave origins, Hagar rose to prominence due to the virtue that most defined her: taqwa. This is to say that, in spite of their slave origins, both these historical figures were liberated from the social bondage of their class and were able to attain symbolic significance within the Islamic tradition, precisely because of their deep-seated faith in God. Hagar's symbolic importance is enshrined in the ritual of hajj, while that of Bilal is embodied in the call to prayer: two rituals whose very purpose is the strengthening of God consciousness. Hagar's worthiness of receiving a divine mission then is without question.

Hagar: A Symbol of Taqwa

Hagar was entrusted by God not simply to give birth to a prophet; her divine instruction entailed much more than childbirth. She is not called "the mother of the Arabs" by Muslim exegetes simply because she was directly related to two prophets—as the wife of Abraham and the mother of Isma'il.[13] Rather, Hagar herself was a God-appointed messenger; and like all messengers of Islam, she endured many trials during her mission, all of which began after her migration to Mecca. The result of her struggles was nothing short of the birth of an entire civilization. The story of Hagar's migration to Mecca, which is narrated in the works of both Ibn Kathir and al-Bawwab, is crucial to understanding how her taqwa enabled her to endure her trials as messenger.

Both exegetes relate that after Isma'il's birth, the Prophet Ibrahim relocated Hagar and his suckling son to a remote place in the desert, not coincidentally the site of what later became the Holy Ka'bah.

> When Prophet Abraham turned to leave Hagar and Isma'il in the desert, Hagar quickly clung to his robe demanding, "Oh Abraham, where are you going, leaving us here without any people or sustenance?" He gave no reply. When she asked again and found he would not reply, she asked, "Is this ordained by God?" After Abraham replied yes, Hagar faithfully answered, "God will not let us die then."[14]

Her initial panic and fear of being left alone with her infant son in a remote desert, without any company and only a bag full of dates and some water, was quickly transformed into relief and acceptance by her awareness of God's presence and her faith in His divine plan. And it is this type of constancy and God consciousness that characterizes Hagar's desert life after Abraham left them to fend for themselves, though not without a prayer to God to sustain his family (14:37).[15] Abraham's prayer was indeed answered, but not without Hagar's suffering.

It is reported that when the water that Abraham left had run out, Hagar could no longer bear looking at her child aching from hunger and thirst. Walking tirelessly between the mountains of Safa and Marwah in search of help for her weary child, she persisted until she had done this seven times. On her last walk up the mountain of Marwah, Hagar heard a voice. She found herself face to face with the archangel Gabriel, who scraped the dust with his wing until the spring of Zamzam gushed forth. From this, Hagar built a dam to contain the water lest it flow away, and she drank and gave drink to Isma'il. In fact, the more Hagar drank from Zamzam, the more the spring gushed forth water.[16]

Reminiscent of Mary, Hagar was nourished by God through divine intervention. Yet such intervention on the part of the Almighty resulted not simply from Hagar's prayers but more importantly from her efforts to find help on her own. This is to say that activism and self-initiation are integral aspects of taqwa, not simply passive faith in God. That God answered Hagar's prayer for sustenance by providing her with the "primordial spring" of Zamzam is not only evidence of her steadfast belief but also its acceptance by the Almighty. Indeed, Hagar exemplifies the notion of active taqwa—a notion not coincidentally enshrined in the prophetic saying, "Tie [your camel] and then rely upon God" ('Aqilha wa 'tawakul).[17]

The spring of Zamzam, moreover, was not only a source of sustenance for Abraham's family, it was also a symbol of fertility brought to Mecca from God as a result of Hagar's suffering and perseverance. Hagar, after all, was assured by the archangel Gabriel that she should not fear, that the place in which she and Isma'il dwelt would be the site of the House of God, soon to be built by her son and his father, and finally that God would not disappoint the People of the House (ahl al-bayt).[18] Here we see the relationship between God and Hagar, or better yet, Creator and messenger, develop even further. Hagar's steadfastness was again answered by God, but here with the promise that her suffering was part of God's larger plan. It was revealed to her that her son, to whom she was so dedicated, was divinely appointed to help his father build the Ka'bah, the quintessential symbol of both monotheism (tawhid) and taqwa. Thanks to Zamzam, moreover, the area of Mecca where Hagar dwelt was now transformed to a fertile valley, which attracted a group of travelers on their way to Greater Syria. Having been generously granted drink from the spring by Hagar, the travelers eventually settled with Hagar and her son in Mecca, and later Isma'il married one of them.[19]

What is equally if not more noteworthy is that Hagar's exhaustive search for help in walking seven times between Safa and Marwah later became "rites" of God, or sha'a'ir, as indicated in the Qur'an.[20] That is, the sha'a'ir that were originated by Hagar in an act of motherly and religious devotion became constitutive parts of what would later be revealed as one of the five pillars of Islam, namely the major pilgrimage (hajj), as well as part of the minor pilgrimage ('umrah). What better way to accept the sacrifice of a faithful servant than to deem that servant's acts of sacrifice as rituals designed to heighten God consciousness in the believers. That God would send revelation vindicating Hagar's rituals when the symbolic monuments of Safa and Marwah were later defiled by the sixth-century pagan Arabs, who placed a male and a female idol near them, is a clear sign of His acceptance of her sacrifice. The Qur'anic verse reads:

> Behold! Safa and Marwah are among the symbols of Allah. So if those who visit the House in the season or at other times, should compass them round, there is no sin in them. And if any one obeys his own impulse to God—be sure that God is He Who recognizes and knows. (2:158)[21]

Not surprisingly, when Hagar died, she was buried in the crescent-shaped tomb adjacent to the Ka'bah (al-Hijr) and within the area of its circumambulation (tawaf). When Isma'il died, he was buried in the same place.[22] Thus, celebrated in a specific ritual of the pilgrimage, "the running (*sa'y*)," Hagar is one of the pillars of Islamic consciousness.[23]

In sum, Hagar symbolizes the strength and courage of God's chosen agents, here in the role of both matriarch and messenger in God's sacred history.[24] Her maternal strength, her courage, constancy, and self-initiative as messenger—all derived from her taqwa—provided her with the necessary qualities not only to fulfill her sacred mission but also to become an aspect of the mission itself. In her suffering for God's cause, Hagar had to endure the distress and danger that have typically marked the careers of God's chosen historical agents. Like God's prophets, moreover, Hagar persevered, and thus her name and memory came to be part of Islam's sacred history and ritual.[25]

Modern Reformers, Hagarian Style

What could modern Muslim women possibly have in common with an Egyptian slave who received divine instruction, gave birth to a prophet, and dwelt in a desert centuries ago? In a word, much. For, it is not the sacred mission or the physical circumstances in which Hagar lived that makes her experiences similar to those of modern women. Rather, it is the way in which she dealt with her struggles and problems, and how she carved out a female presence within Islamic orthodoxy in the process. More specifically, Hagar framed her struggles within an Islamic mindset where monotheism (tawhid) and God consciousness (taqwa) constituted the basis for her sacred mission in the first place. This mindset for Hagar was key in fighting the wrongs of pagan society. That is, her taqwa inspired her to work actively to establish God's plan. It defined how her reality was forged as well as how the obstacles to that reality were leveled. It is precisely this taqwa that has molded Muslim women into leaders. Before turning to a discussion of how three modern women reformers integrate their God-centeredness into their modern-day struggles in ways reminiscent of Hagar, it is only fitting to examine briefly the concept of Islamic leadership in order to better understand the contribution these women make as Muslim leaders.

Problematizing Islamic Leadership

Is there a difference between Islamic leadership and *female* Islamic leadership? When we speak of Islamic leadership and female Islamic leadership, are we speaking in dichotomous terms, as though the first expression denotes a male bastion of activity, and the second a leadership exclusively for females? Is Islamic leadership, in short, gendered? In principle, there are forms of Islamic leadership that are not fundamentally gender specific with respect to which sex can or must exercise authority within a community—for example, narrating a tradition of the Prophet. Practically speaking, however, traditional Islam has historically apportioned most forms of leadership to men, leaving women only a few leadership roles. Men, for example, have retained the right to lead congregational prayers, while women have historically retained the right to testify as single witnesses in issues related to women, such as childbirth.

Yet herein lies the problem with this scheme of Islamic leadership. Despite the range of legitimate leadership possibilities in theory, leadership as it has come to be exercised in Muslim communities both within and outside the United States follows this early tradition. That is, in issues related to larger Islam, males have retained the right to lead the community; in issues related to women, women have retained the right to speak publicly for other women. In fact, "Islamic leadership" comes to represent the invisible construct, certainly assumed to be masculine, to which the qualifier "female" must be added in order to shift the focus from larger issues of Islam to issues exclusive to women. Put simply, in those situations in which a woman becomes a Muslim leader in a Muslim community, she is a leader largely, if not solely, because of her activism concerning women's issues; her leadership is very rarely accepted as contributing to larger issues of Islam.[26] This type of leadership reifies a traditional Muslim gender regime—or a set of social rules that relegate one set of activities to men and another to women—so that women feel socially compelled to legitimate their activism by focusing on traditional women's issues (education, social work, and the like). Clearly in this scheme, the notion of Islamic leadership itself is quite gendered.

An examination of the works of three Muslim women demonstrates that, while their leadership is certainly derived from their pioneering works that tackle female issues in Muslim communities head on, more importantly, they use the authority of Islamic sacred scripture to contribute to Islamic orthodoxy itself, by arguing for gender equality. "Gender jihad,"[27] or struggle in the name of God toward socially recognized and institutionalized gender parity, forces a reconfiguration of the traditional Islamic paradigm—not because it pits the category of woman against that of man but precisely for the opposite reason. Gender jihad seeks greater complementarity between the sexes, as based on the Qur'an. Gender jihad, in short, is a struggle for gender parity in Muslim society in the name of divine justice. It is a struggle to end a long-standing gender regime that has paralyzed Muslim women, preventing them from becoming Muslim leaders without having to add the qualifier "female" or "woman."

In fact, gender jihad—which all three of these women undertake—calls into question the very legitimacy of Islamic leadership as a male-dominated sphere of activity. Their work changes the playing field and the game-book definition of who qualifies as a player, of who can be a legitimate Muslim leader. Simply put, in changing the paradigm of how we talk about gender in Islam, the contributions of these women force a change in the way in which we speak about Islam in general, and Islamic leadership in particular.

Wadudian Hermeneutics

The first model of Islamic leadership is evident in the work of Amina Wadud, a professor of Islamic studies in the Department of Philosophy and Religious Studies at Virginia Commonwealth University. As an African American, Wadud, like many American converts, sought refuge in Islam from the many social contradictions within American society. After converting, however, she quickly came to see that "Islam" and "Muslim" do not always mean the same thing and that practice lagged far behind theory, particularly when it came to gender parity within Muslim communities. To address this crucial problem, in the late 1980s as a graduate student at the University of Michigan, Wadud began the initial research for what would become the pioneering work, *Qur'an and Woman: Rereading the Sacred Text from a Woman's Perspective*. Since its publication in Malaysia in 1992, *Qur'an and Woman* has been translated into Bhasa Indonesian (in 1994) and Turkish (in 1997), and it occupied first place on a best-seller list in a Muslim newspaper in South Africa in 1994.[28]

Wadud's book does not treat the topic of Islam and women, nor is it a book about Muslim women. Rather, Wadud develops a new hermeneutical approach to reading the Qur'an that is female inclusive. She addresses the concept of woman, not in the fragmentary way in which other commentators have extracted verses of the Qur'an about women and interpreted them in isolation from the rest of the Qur'an. Rather, Wadud proposes an interpretive methodology based on the absolute monotheism or unity of God (tawhid), and whereby the unity of the Qur'an or God's Word permeates all of its parts, so that verses on woman fall into a larger holistic framework of the Qur'an's coherence, or the Qur'anic weltanschauung.

For example, in interpreting the first verse of the Qur'anic chapter entitled "Women," which treats the creation of Adam and Eve, Wadud philologically deconstructs four key concepts (*ayat* means a divine sign; *min* is the preposition "from"; *nafs* refers to the soul; and *zawj* is translated as mate) found in this verse and relates them to their usage throughout the Qur'an.[29] Applied to the narrative of creation, Wadud's hermeneutics render a different reading of Eve than that posited by traditional exegetes, who relied on biblical tradition since Qur'anic revelation on this issue is ambiguous or silent.[30] Eve in this reading was created *from* the same neuter *soul* as Adam and thus became Adam's *mate* —or in Qur'anic terms, the other congruent half of the pair (*zawj*), for the Qur'an very clearly states that everything in creation is paired. Given this reading, it is Qur'anically justified to argue that Eve was not born from the "crooked bone" of Adam, as the traditional exegetes state. Indeed, the "crooked bone" hadith, found in the authentic collection of Bukhari, raises a sensitive and even controversial question about those ahadith deemed "genuine" that clearly contradict the Qur'anic intent of gender equality.[31] Thus, instead of starting with a flawed female prototype, humanity descends from a Qur'anically vindicated Eve who is Adam's gender equal by virtue of a gender-neutral soul that God breathes into all humanity equally. Eve is thus physically and spiritually perfected, like Adam, to become God's vicegerent.[32]

Because women were nearly excluded from the foundational discourse that established the traditional paradigm for what it means to be Muslim, women have ultimately been relegated to the role of subject, but without agency.[33] Though it has silenced women in the interpretive process, this discourse, argues Wadud, has defined what voice the Qur'an itself has given to women. She says: "In the final analysis, the creation of the basic paradigms through which we examine and discuss the Qur'an and Qur'anic interpretation was generated without the participation and first representation of women. Their voicelessness during critical periods of development in Qur'anic interpretation has not gone unnoticed, but it has been mistakenly equated with voicelessness in the text itself."[34]

By excluding the female voice in scriptural or religious commentary, Muslim exegetes end up talking about Muslim women as subjects while inscribing their own (male) experiences onto the female subject in the interpretive process. What Wadud attempts to rectify, then, is twofold. First, she relies exclusively on the Qur'an to establish definitive criteria for evaluating the differences between "text" and "context" (between what is intended in the Qur'an and what is actually practiced in Muslim society). Armed with these criteria, she argues for the intended reading of the text particularly in those instances where Muslim contexts have failed to reach the Qur'anic intent—which, more often than not, fall in the domain of gender equality.

Second, again with these Qur'anic criteria in hand, Wadud is able to challenge the tenets of Islamic thought that grant primacy to males over females in favor of a more gender-equal paradigm. It is not enough for modern Qur'anic commentators to simply "add women and stir," or integrate the subject of woman into the interpretive process while ignoring her agency. Wadud shows that a hermeneutical approach to interpreting woman in the Qur'an must include women as active agents in both the intellectual and physical creation of a just social order. In challenging the traditional paradigm, she reimbues woman with her full humanity and moral agency as God-appointed vicegerent (*khalifah*)—as is directly stated in the Qur'an—while she creates a niche for a female interpretive presence. In the process, woman regains her lost agency in the Islamic interpretive process; she is now both subject and agent instead of subject without agency.

In linking Qur'anic ideas, syntactical structures, principles, or themes together into one holistic methodology, Wadud's hermeneutical approach as a Qur'anic methodology is not entirely new. Her work follows in a long tradition of modernist scriptural commentary (*tafsir*), though it tends to fall within the aims of new Qur'anic epistemologies, not to be confused with the classical approach to Qur'anic commentary.[35] While the aim of all tafsir is to disclose the Qur'an's norms to the faithful, to explicate in detail how they are called to discern truth and achieve goodness, modernity has inspired new and different approaches to the problematic of the Qur'an's eternal nature versus its day-to-day cultural specificity (approaches that are most often now written in the form of theoretical treatises rather than Qur'anic commentary).[36] Following modernist scholars who have sought reform based on the value system of the Qur'an as a whole in order to derive new guidance consonant with the present, Wadud assumes the right to individual interpretation of scripture (*ijtihad*) by differentiating between two textual levels in the Qur'an. These are the historically and culturally contextualized "prior text" and the wider "megatext" of essential or culturally universal relevance.[37] Put simply, like modernist theologians and scholars before her, Wadud bases her Qur'anic hermeneutics on the critical distinction between the universals and particulars of the Qur'an.

What is new about Wadud's work is her attempt to pursue an answer to "the woman question" exclusively by examining the concept of woman in the Qur'an, an approach that, she argues, "turned out to be nearly unprecedented throughout fourteen centuries of Islamic thought."[38] Wadud emphasizes "how a Qur'anic hermeneutics that is inclusive of female experiences and of the female voice could yield greater gender justice to Islamic thought and contribute toward the achievement of that justice in Islamic praxis."[39] By differentiating between two textual levels of the Qur'an, namely, the universal and particular, *then* inserting both the ontological woman and the female exegete within this very approach, Wadud reforms a pre-existing hermeneutics to be gender sensitive in content and gender inclusive in application. In making this distinction of textual "readings," she is methodologically justified in arguing that gender distinctions based on early Arabian precedent are superseded by the Qur'an's emphasis on gender equality.[40] Wadud in sum offers her work as a contribution, one that is uniquely female inclusive, to the larger historical corpus of Qur'anic exegesis. Like Hagar, she carves out female space within Islamic ritual, here of scriptural interpretation. In contributing this new hermeneutical model, Wadud is essentially expanding an intellectual legacy that dates back centuries by moving beyond this legacy.

Sonbol's Fatwas

The second model of Islamic leadership can be found in the work of Amira Sonbol, a professor of Islamic history at Georgetown University's Center for Muslim-Christian Understanding. Born and raised in Egypt, Sonbol settled in the United States after completing her doctorate in Middle East history at Georgetown University in the early 1980s.

In her *Women, the Family, and Divorce Laws in Islamic History* (1996), Sonbol, together with several other historians, challenges a number of critical concepts related to women, Islamic law, and the coming of modernity to Muslim society.[41] Sonbol sets out in this volume to challenge Western perceptions of Muslim women based on longstanding preconceptions that Islam is *necessarily* inimical to women's rights. One need only recall that, of all the historical discourses on "the veil," all of which have falsely served to define Muslim women's status, the one that stands out most in the Western imagination depicts the veil as Islam's way of keeping Muslim women oppressed, enslaved, passive, and illiterate. The power of social discourse is indeed far reaching, even when it is not based in any historical reality.

To counter such misleading perceptions of Islam and Muslim women, Sonbol and her colleagues examine seventeenth-, eighteenth-, and nineteenth-century documents of the Islamic law (*shari'ah*) courts with fresh eyes, new research methods, and new language skills. In the process, the volume has set new standards of scholarship on this topic.[42] Central to its findings is a conclusion that has taken many by surprise. While Islamic law has historically proven flexible and advantageous to Muslim women, modern legal reform, which was introduced into Muslim countries as nationally applied secular and European-modeled "rational" laws, has not inspired positive changes in the legal status of Muslim women. Sonbol argues that "The shari'ah that came into being after the modernization of law and the reform of courts differed from the previous one in that it was designed to favor the new hegemonic order coming to power as part of the nation-state structure. It is a mistake to believe that the shari'ah code applied by nation-states in the modern period is simply a vestige of the past and hence to regard the traditional laws as the cause of the present subjugation of women, when in fact the causes of subjugation are located in the modern reforms and the handling of personal laws."[43] That is, this volume directly tackles the question of whether Islamic law really is inimical, by its very nature, to women's rights by looking at how Islamic law was actually interpreted and applied in historical societies.

Contrary to the common assumption that the shari'ah is inimical to Muslim women, these scholars find that Muslim women of different Muslim countries were historically better positioned and had more power to influence personal status laws within the legal system when the law was based on the more flexible and evolving system of Islamic jurisprudence, rather than the rigidly codified secular law. To provide historical proof, Sonbol treats the issue of gender violence.[44] She is particularly interested in the impact on Egyptian women's lives of legal reforms in the modern period. Rape (which was recognized as rape, or *ightisab*, in premodern Islamic courts and was dealt with accordingly) was in the modern period codified, not under personal status laws where Islamic law was applied but rather under criminal law where secular codes were applied. As a result of this change in legal codification, judges followed modern laws that were more lenient toward rape, and often preferred to deal with such cases under different titles that made the offense more acceptable.

Writing elsewhere on the issue of wifely obedience to the husband (*ta'ah*) under nineteenth-century marriage contracts, Sonbol similarly concludes that the policies applied and the conditions laid down for marriage by the state were really based on new laws established as part of nation-state building, and not on Ottoman-style shari'ah. For, argues Sonbol, the modern judge has been given new powers; it was formerly his prerogative to force the wife to remain with her husband if he did not agree with her reasons for a divorce. But state laws have gone much further than that; they actually give the husband full right to his wife's "person," physically, sexually and mentally. The state has become an instrument by which a wife is delivered legally through the courts and, until very recently, physically delivered by the police into custody of her husband. The new coercive measures have also defined a new institution to ensure a husband's right to his wife. This is known as *bayt al-ta'ah*, unheard of before the last decades of the nineteenth century.[45]

It was precisely this "pick and choose" method employed by modern judges when using Islamic jurisprudence (*fiqh*) sources that "added state power to male-biological power to ensure the superior control by men over women. In this the state acted as a male patriarch, extending and enforcing male-power."[46] Thus, the secular legal codes that were established in the twentieth century constrained personal status laws, which ultimately proved less "progressive" than modernization, theoretical works contend.

Underlying this argument is a challenge to the theoretical viewpoint that sees modernity, modernization, and the West as *necessarily* "progressive" for Muslim women, and Islamic law as backward and oppressive, especially for women. In fact, this volume directly attacks modernization theory by showing its methodological limitations. In order to prove that Islam presently subjugates women, studies grounded in modernization theory rely exclusively on historical *textual* proof by looking at traditional commentary from the Qur'an, Prophetic sayings (ahadith), Islamic jurisprudence (fiqh), and other religious texts. Such studies never examine the *actual* contexts to see if these religious texts reflected historical reality. Like Wadud, then, Sonbol differentiates between the interpretive text and historical context, but with a significant difference in meaning.[47] In making this crucial distinction, Sonbol finds that the actual lives of Muslim women in premodern Muslim societies were freer and less oppressed than the religious text would suggest, precisely because fiqh was not static or inflexible. Rather, such law was constantly being reinterpreted to meet the challenges that confronted women. This is not to suggest that modernization had no positive impact on Muslim women. As Sonbol acknowledges, "There is no question that modernization has changed the situation of Muslim women dramatically and that the status of women has become one of greater openness and less seclusion. However, it should be emphasized that women in premodern Islamic society were quite dynamic and participated in decisions regarding legal and personal status . . . [however] the historical transformations of the last two centuries, although allowing women a greater public role, actually brought about a general deterioration in social maneuverability, especially for women."[48]

It is this argument—that Islamic law was more flexible and malleable in addressing women's grievances in this period than during the modern period, when it was constrained by the encroaching nation-state —that clashed with the received scholarly wisdom at the time of the book's publication. This has made the volume a real contribution, epistemologically and methodologically, to Middle East history and women's studies, as Elizabeth Fernea confirms: "This is what Amira Sonbol is doing in her work, looking backward and forward in time at women's legal and economic position. New research methods, new language skills, new scholars, often women like Sonbol herself, are beginning to change the way Middle Eastern history is viewed, to animate and deepen serious women's studies across the globe. This is a hopeful and encouraging trend."[49] Indeed, Sonbol's volume posits and proves an alternative paradigm, which constitutes a real sea change in scholarship on women and Islamic law.

Sonbol goes beyond reevaluating the historical past to vindicate Islam's alleged single-handed role in subjugating women in academic scholarship, though this task is itself noteworthy. Because of her extensive knowledge of shari'ah, she has engaged in the interpretive process itself, here in the realm of Islamic legal formulations. She embarks on a mission similar to that of Wadud, namely, to formulate a female-inclusive interpretation of the Qur'an, particularly of the chapter on women (*Surat al-Nisa'*).[50] Like Wadud, Sonbol draws from the works of Muslim medieval exegetes, as well as contemporary conservative scholars, in order to show the limitations of such a discourse, particularly in light of contemporary changes in Muslims' social contexts, values, and thinking. Instead, through her own re-reading of this Qur'anic chapter, she arrives at a more gender-equal idea of woman with the aim of making Islam more relevant, especially to women. Integral to her reading—and even that of Wadud—is the attempt to place the Qur'an in its rightful place as *the* primary source of Islamic legal formulations, which implies a concomitant de-emphasis of ahadith and israiliyyat that either contradict or have no basis in the Qur'an. That is, in upholding the authority of the Qur'an in determining what is Islamic, Sonbol endows her own read-ing with a legitimacy that poses a biting challenge to established andro-centric interpretations that are based heavily on nondivine sources.

Furthermore, Sonbol's gender jihad has influenced legal reform. Her scholarship has affected other women, as evidenced in their crusade to change rape laws in Egypt, and contributed to discussions of legal re-form in Jordan. Through her scholarly work and discussions with Mus-lim women, Sonbol has shown that many of the laws within the Egyp-tian legal system came from French, not Islamic, laws; unlike the French legal codes, for example, Islamic law did not protect a rapist from pun-ishment. Thanks in part to her scholarship, Egypt is now changing its laws so that rape is punishable by death, whereas previously only gang rapists were sentenced to death. In sum, Sonbol contributes through her scripturo-legal interpretations a perspective of Muslim women, Muslim societies, and Islamic law that challenges the long-standing authority of archaic academic methodologies, Muslim exegetical commentaries, and contemporary Islamic legal formulations alike. In the process, she con-tributes her perspective to a legacy of Islamic law in hopes of expanding the parameters of Islamic legal orthodoxy.

Alkhateeb: A Modern Kind of Leader

The third and final model of Islamic leadership is showcased in the im-pressive activism of Sharifa Alkhateeb. Born in Philadelphia to a Yemeni father and Czechoslovakian mother, Alkhateeb was raised exclusively in the United States. She received a bachelor's degree in English litera-ture from the University of Pennsylvania and a master's in comparative religion from Norwich University. She is currently vice-president of the National American Council for Muslim Women (NACMW) after serving as its president upon its creation in 1983.

The council was created out of Muslim women's disillusionment and alienation in American Muslim organizations that have been led pre-dominantly by men. Like Wadud and Sonbol, then, Alkhateeb seeks a niche for a female presence that is not mediated by male interpreters. "Defining what is Islamic," argues Alkhateeb, "is a matter that must include women."[51] In helping to found the NACMW, Alkhateeb validated Muslim women's experiences by creating a forum to discuss women's issues while offering an Islamic solution. More importantly, however, NACMW encouraged women to acquire more Islamic knowledge as a way to gain greater control over their lives. That is, this organization's very raison d'être is not necessarily to address problems as a community of women; rather, it is to train each individual woman to be her own person. To this end, NACMW's objectives include "educating Muslim women about Islam from original sources, helping women develop and act upon their own self-concept, helping women become confident and strong as individuals and as members of their families, and helping women to connect to the larger American society in a contributory way."[52]

Many members of NACMW are converts or immigrants who have acquired their knowledge of Islam second and third hand; many do not read the Qur'an directly. Thus educating these women in basic Islamic knowledge is essential to achieving these goals. "Once the knowledge level of women is raised," says Alkhateeb, "their consciousness and thus their self-concept will be raised to such a level as to preclude anyone suppressing, misusing, or limiting their growth."[53]

By encouraging women to interact directly with the Qur'anic text, NACMW attempts to empower them to change the unfortunate realities in which they often live, realities that many times are created by their own ignorance of Islamic scripture. For example, many members of NACMW entered the organization unaware that, under Islamic law, the money they earned was self-entitled money that did not have to go, by legal right, toward maintaining the home. Through training programs, Qur'anic study circles, and written publications, NACMW teaches women how to translate their new knowledge of the Qur'an and Islam into the most basic Islamic social skills. For example, NACMW members are taught how to talk to a husband or family member without compromising their own individual opinion or how to create a gender-balanced marriage contract. In teaching women to be their own person, NACMW seeks to undo long-standing traditions that have kept Muslim women handicapped in the name of Islam, by teaching them how to Qur'anically contest authority without *necessarily* being rebellious against God.

Equally important, the organization has not shied away from controversial issues like domestic violence (including sexual, verbal, and psychological abuse). It was the first national Muslim organization to make domestic violence and violence against children a topic of a national conference. Thus, NACMW has challenged the traditional model of Muslim organizations in America, not only because it is female led and constituted, but also because of the sensitive issues it openly addresses. In fact, in 1993 NACMW, under the presidency of Alkhateeb, conducted a survey about violence against women that included questions never before asked in a Muslim public survey.[54] In addition to educating women about Islam, NACMW encourages Muslim women to be active in the public sphere. Significant in this regard is NACMW's assistance in securing low-interest loans for Muslim women interested in embarking on economic pursuits. That women's presence in the community is an Islamic obligation is central to creating a gender-equal Muslim social order.

In addition to NACMW, Alkhateeb has been involved in an impressive array of activities—a reflection of her wide-ranging "gender jihad." In 1994 she convened a national retreat to study the connection between the International Convention on the Elimination of All Forms of Discrimination against Women (CEDAW) and the Qur'an and hadith, which ultimately led to the founding of the Muslim Women's Georgetown Study Project. The project was created specifically to prepare for a panel at the United Nations Fourth World Conference on Women in Beijing, China. In its preparations, the group under the leadership of Alkhateeb discussed issues such as economic justice, female genital mutilation, and basic health care for women. It is noteworthy that NACMW as an independent organization was involved in five panel discussions at the Beijing conference. Finally, in 1998, Alkhateeb presented a paper on Islam and girls' education at the first world conference on women sponsored by the White House and the U. S. Agency for International Development. In fact, she is often consulted by the White House on matters pertaining to Islam and Muslim women, and has been instrumental in challenging prevalent misconceptions about Islam on Capitol Hill (misconceptions such as Islam condones radicalism and terrorism).

Alkhateeb's activism is not limited to women's issues; she is also interested in correcting myths about Middle Eastern culture. She has taught Middle Eastern culture as an intercultural trainer of teachers in the Fairfax County (Virginia) public schools. She was also a producer and host to a television program titled "Middle Eastern Parenting," designed to help bridge the gap between home and school for parents of Middle Eastern backgrounds. Clearly, Alkhateeb through her activism —and primarily through education—has attempted to change the paradigm of how Islamic leadership itself is socially manifested by providing a model of female leadership inspired by the Qur'an.

Women as Modern Islamic Reformers

How do these female models of Islamic leadership hark back to the reform model of Hagar? First and foremost, these women's God consciousness inspires their individual sacred missions, for active taqwa engenders a type of thinking about God and his intended plan that often translates into a mission of social reform. Islam, after all, has witnessed for centuries the coming and going of countless Muslim reformers seeking to make Islam more consonant with contemporary life, precisely because their faith in God and the initiative that faith inspires prompt such individuals—regardless of sex—to establish God's will on earth. The establishment of divine will necessitates public activism and even leadership. That women can and should be counted among these reformers is demonstrated by the type of woman reformer presented here. Just as Hagar's faith inspired her to struggle to establish God's will in a pagan patriarchal society, so does the faith of these women inspire them to embark upon a jihad of gender aimed at correcting the misogynist ideas and behaviors that plague Muslim communities today. Here liberation is sought exclusively by access to the divine, for all these women look solely to God for answers about how to establish his will. While their sex certainly may have contributed to the type of mission they undertook, their jihad for reform hinges, not on being a woman but on the single feature that distinguishes all of humanity in God's eyes, namely, one's level of faith (taqwa).

A second characteristic these women share with their archetypal ancestor is that—as a result of their reform efforts aimed at the establishment of God's plan—they, like Hagar, have carved out a female presence not simply within public space in Muslim communities, but also and more importantly within divine space, or Islamic orthodoxy. It is not simply because these women venture into the public sphere that I isolate them as new models of Islamic leadership; it is rather that their struggles for God's cause produce a real change in Islamic worship. As Hagar's struggles were accepted by the Almighty and were consequently enshrined within the Islamic ritual of hajj, their struggles produce an equally noteworthy result by creating a female role in the scriptural and legal interpretive process of how to worship. Each creates a paradigm of self, or model of individual identity of a woman, that ultimately renegotiates the paradigm of collective self, or model of collective identity as a community. In reforming women's issues, in sum, these women end up reforming Islam in unprecedented ways.[55]

This raises the question, What do these women and their works share that makes them new models of Islamic leadership? First, they contest the status quo of gender inequality by shaking the very foundations of knowledge, of what constitutes "Truth." They have created an epistemological shift whereby religious knowledge, rather than being understood as authoritative and incontestable, is revealed to be constructed, value laden, and context specific. In the process, they dismantle the traditional androcentric paradigms that have excluded woman from the interpretive process. They produce instead new kinds of knowledge, female-inclusive knowledge about Islam that is protected by the Qur'anic principle of gender equality. After all, for these women, scriptural interpretations and legal formulations of the Qur'an that are not gender inclusive are not comprehensive of God's message and hence the comprehensiveness is itself compromised.

Because their call for gender jihad is based on the Qur'an, these women imbue their sacred missions with a religious authority that cannot easily be contested or dismissed by the more conservative Muslim community. In contesting old paradigms, moreover, these women provide a blueprint for other women to follow. Elizabeth Fernea, in her travels around the globe, encountered increasing numbers of Muslim women who are contesting outdated and paternalistic religious traditions: "Everywhere I found women reordering their activities to meet new challenges from the old order. The tradition of God the Father, the tradition that men rule, is the order faced by all women who have inherited the paternalistic, monotheistic religious tradition of Judaism, Christianity, and Islam. This tradition is now being contested on a daily basis as women move into the public workforce beside men, and expect recognition, respect and power."[56]

That these female-inclusive Islamic formulations have emerged in American society is related, in many ways, to postmodernist thought, which has allowed Muslims to be critical of Islamic practices in ways that may not yet be possible in less politically open Muslim states. In fact, as scholars like Ali Mazrui argue, American secular society provides fertile grounds for a brand of Islam that is unfettered by cultural baggage that comes from Muslim countries.[57] Sonbol puts it best in saying,

Islam as a religion and a movement also has a lot to learn from America, freedom and individual rights are at the heart of American idealism. There is nothing in Islam to stand against such ideals and we as American Muslims can contribute a lot to our communities by leaning toward such ideals in our interpretations. Since law is so central to Islam as it is to the modern world, it makes sense for me as a modern Muslim woman and a historian to direct my work toward correcting the wrong impressions of the past, to deconstruct what they tell us is "truth" to come to fundamental and basic rights. The contribution of society can be shown through a study of historical context, and once it is clear where God's word begins and society takes over, then we can see how and when knowledge was constructed.[58]

Because Muslims in America (whether of immigrant or American origin) must formulate an Islam that makes sense to an American Muslim lifestyle, more often than not, cultural ideas of Islam imported to the United States from various Muslim countries are set aside. In such a context, where Muslims constitute a minority under secular rule, not only are Muslim women able to develop and put into action their thoughts on Islam, they are free to export them back to Muslim countries to effect change even in those communities.

In the process of decentering traditional religious knowledge and appropriating the written word, these leadership models make a number of noteworthy contributions to Muslim women and Islam. First, women regain lawful access to scripture, law, and education—the three crucial areas that authorize a Muslim to be a leader. And by gaining access to these three areas, Muslim women can reestablish their individual relationship with God without the mediation of male interpreters. A crucial consequence of this increased access to scripture is nothing short of the rise of various movements for legal reform, particularly in traditional divorce practices and the laws of inheritance.[59] A woman can thus lead herself as well as serve as a leader to men, as Hagar did in her own sacred mission while leading Isma'il to fulfill his own. Equally significant is that Islamic leadership no longer remains exclusively in the hands of Muslim men, and the qualifiers "female" or "woman" are no longer necessary to shift the discussion to women's issues. Men and women as gender equals have equal claim to authority since there is equal access to those power sources that legitimate authority. Just as with Hagar, whose sacrifices were accepted by God and even enshrined within Islamic rituals, these women's jihad within gender issues has changed the face of Islam itself, at least in America. Wadud, Sonbol, and Alkhateeb, by example, have not only inspired other women to seize their right to help define what is Islamic, they have made Islam more pluralistic. These women are not alone in this endeavor, as Barbara Stowasser has wisely noted.[60]

Second, Wadud, Sonbol, and Alkhateeb have challenged not only the received wisdom of Islamic orthodoxy but also what has been left unsaid. Controversial issues like gender violence are scarcely spoken of in Muslim communities. Their willingness to bring these issues into the spotlight reflects their commitment to tackle social ills caused by gender inequality, even at the risk of being marginalized within the Muslim community. Finally, while these women accept the Islamic legacy they have inherited as Muslims, and as Muslim women in particular, they have sought through their works to stay within this tradition but also move beyond it in order to meet the modern challenges to Islam.

Stowasser observes, "The contemporary age has produced a new Islamic epistemology in which scripture-sanctioned gender paradigms play an important role."[61] Indeed, change also came with the modern age and its modernist and reformist scholars.[62] Included in this group are the women presented here. They are developing their own spiritual link to God as individual servants, now through direct scriptural access, and becoming leaders in their own right through their efforts to reform society. In uncovering what was essentially a silent yet defining dimension of Hagar's significance in the Islamic exegetical tradition, this chapter has attempted to narrate the story of female Islamic consciousness (taqwa) and its continued centrality to Muslim women's modern-day missions aimed at correcting the wrongs found in contemporary patriarchal Muslim communities. The taqwa that Hagar so nicely enshrined manifests itself differently in modern women—that is, as gender jihad—yet it produces similar results: namely, the carving out of divine space for the female agent of God whose reform is based on establishing God's plan. That is, by examining the works of three pioneering women, we find striking parallels to Hagar's narrative of reform and liberation; for Muslim women can, through their struggles in the name of God, find a place equal to men within Islamic orthodoxy. Indeed, the feminine is not only very much part and parcel of Islam, it has the potential to contribute to its very orthodoxy. We only have to look deep enough and in the proper spirit into the Islamic tradition in order to find female religious devotion aimed straight at the doors of heaven.

Notes

1. See Muhammad Ibn Ishaq, *Mukhtasar Sirat Ibn Hisham: al-Sirah al-Nabawiyah* (Beirut: Dar al-Nafais, 1977); al-Tabari, *Tafsir al-Tabari* (Damascus: Dar al-Qalam, 1997); Isma'il ibn Umar Ibn Kathir, *al-Bidayah wa'al-Nihayah* (Cairo: Matba'at al-Sa'adah, 1939).

2. Barbara Freyer Stowasser, *Women in the Qur'an: Traditions and Interpretation* (New York: Oxford University Press, 1994), 47.

3. Ibid., 43.

4. See Patricia Crone and Mark Cohen, *Hagarism: The Making of the Islamic World* (Cambridge: Cambridge University Press, 1977).

5. Notwithstanding the many meanings and historical contexts that the categories Islam, Muslim women, and Islamic leadership invoke, these categories are still useful analytic constructs since they are used here with very specific definitions in mind. When using "Islam," I am speaking exclusively of the religion as understood, interpreted, and practiced in the United States, recognizing that American Islam is only one possible meaning among the different "Islams"

that exist globally. And even within American Islam, there are significant sub-groups. However, for the sake of this chapter, I limit myself to Sunni Orthodox Islam as practiced by the majority of Muslims living in America, whether of immigrant or American origin. Thus, "Muslim women" refers to the female adherents within that majority Muslim group. Finally, "Islamic leaders" refers to those individuals who are socially accepted by their followers as legitimate authorities and who have, in varying degrees, interpretive power to declare what is or is not "Islamic."

6. Traditionalism, or traditional Islam, refers to "the mainstream conservative school of thought that views Islam as an inherited, balanced system of faith and action based on and sanctioned by scripture and its interpretation through the verifying authority of past scholarly consensus" (Barbara Stowasser, "Gender Issues and Contemporary Quran Interpretation," in *Islam, Gender and Social Change*, ed. Yvonne Yazbeck Haddad and John L. Esposito [New York: Oxford University Press, 1998], 37).

7. It is important to note that the ahadith found in the exegetical works of Ibn Kathir cited here and in similar works are not to be confused with the authentic ahadith found in the legitimate hadith collections, like Bukhari. The ahadith found in the exegetical works cited here did not undergo the same rigorous weeding-out process that later came to be called the science of hadith, except for the "crooked bone" hadith mentioned below. Instead, these ahadith constitute part of the commentary of the exegetes, and should be accepted as precarious until proven otherwise. See Muhammad ibn Ismail Bukhari, *Sahih al-Bukhari: The Early Years of Islam* (Gilbraltar: Dar al-Andalus, 1981).

8. Stowasser, *Women in the Qur'an*, 44.

9. Ibid., 67.

10. Ibn Kathir, *al-Bidayah*, 140.

11. Fakhr al-Din Muhammad ibn al-Razi, *al-Tafsir al-Kabir* (Cairo: n.p., 1934–62), 16.

12. The view that Hagar was so named because of the hijrah is not likely since she was named before her migration to Egypt.

13. Sulayman Salim al-Bawwab, *Mi'a Awa'il min al-Nisa* (Damascus: Dar al-Hikmah, 1992), 17; Stowasser cites Ibn Ishaq as calling Hagar "the mother of the Arabs." See Stowasser, *Women in the Qur'an*, 47.

14. Ibn Kathir, *al-Bidayah*, 141; al-Bawwab, *Mi'a Awa'il*, 21.

15. It is commonly understood in Qur'anic commentary that *"dhurriyah,"* meaning "offspring," includes the mother of the offspring, which in this case means that Hagar was included in Abraham's prayer to God cited in this verse.

16. Ibn Kathir, *al-Bidayah*, 143–44; al-Bawwab, *Mi'a Awa'il*, 21. See translation in Stowasser, *Women in the Qur'an*, 47–48.

17. This saying clearly denotes that an individual is to do all that is possible when undertaking an endeavor, putting his or her faith in God thereafter to deliver what is best.

18. The "People of the House," or *ahl al-bayt*, refers in Sunni orthodoxy to

those descendants of Ibrahim from *both* Hagar and Sarah, meaning that the pro-phetic lineages produced by both matriarchs are included. This is evidenced in the Qur'anic use of the expression in 11:17, which refers to Sarah and her lineage as "People of the House," while 14:37 refers to Hagar as ahl al-bayt. See Isma'il ibn Umar Ibn Kathir, *Tafsir Ibn Kathir* (Cairo: Dar al-Hadith, 1990), 433, 521. This definition is not to be confused with the Shi'ite understanding of ahl al-bayt, which refers to the descendants of Prophet Muhammad's daughter, Fatima, and her husband and last caliph, Ali. Inherent within this understanding in Shi'i orthodoxy is the idea that Shi'i leadership (the office of *imam*) must come from a blood descendant of Ali.

19. Ibn Kathir, *al-Bidayah*, 143; al-Bawwab, *Mi'a Awa'il*, 22.

20. See 2:158.

21. The commentary of 2:158 made by Yusuf Ali is noteworthy in this respect: "The virtue of patient perseverance in faith leads to the mention of two symbolic monuments of that virtue. These are the two little hills of Safa and Marwah now absorbed in the city of Makkah, and close to the well of Zamzam. Here, accord-ing to tradition, the lady Hagar, mother of the infant Isma'il, prayed for water in the parched desert, and in her eager quest around these hills, she found her prayer answered and saw the Zamzam spring. Unfortunately the Pagan Arabs had placed a male and a female idol here, and their gross and superstitious rites caused offense to the early Muslims. They felt some hesitation in going round these places during the Pilgrimage. As a matter of fact they should have known that the Ka'bah (the House of Allah) had been itself defiled with idols, and was sanctified again by the purity of Muhammad's life and teaching. The lesson is that the most sacred things may be turned to the base uses; that we are not therefore necessarily to ban a thing misused; that if our intentions and life are pure, Allah will recognize them even if the world cast stones at us because of some evil associations which they join with what we do, or with the people we associate with, or with the places which claim our reverence." See Abdallah Yusuf Ali, *The Holy Qur'an: Text, Translation and Commentary* (Brentwood, Md.: Amana Publications, 1983), 63.

22. Stowasser, *Women in the Qur'an*, 48.

23. Ibid., 47.

24. Ibid., 43.

25. Ibid., 44.

26. There are obvious exceptions to this statement, as evidenced in the rise of female political leaders like Benazir Bhutto. Because this kind of female political leadership (i.e., head of state) occurs rarely when compared with male political leadership and under circumstances very different from the rise of local female leaders in Muslim communities, I do not include these leaders in this study.

27. I borrowed this expression from Amina Wadud, *Qur'an and Woman: Re-reading the Sacred Text from a Woman's Perspective* (New York: Oxford University Press, 1999). The definition used here is based on my own understanding of the borrowed expression.

28. Ibid., xvi.

29. *Ayah* (pl. *ayat*) is "a sign" or set of empirical signs that can be perceived by humankind, and that are Qur'anically intended to help complete the purpose of the Book by providing guidance to humankind. *Min* is used for the English preposition "from" to imply the extraction of a thing from other thing(s); it also means "of the same nature as." *Nafs* has both a common and technical usage. The common usage translates as "self" (and its plural, *anfus,* as "selves"), and it is never used in the Qur'an with reference to any created self other than humankind. The technical usage of the term refers to the common origin of all humankind. Finally, *zawj* is used in the Qur'an to mean "mate," "spouse," or "group," and its plural *azwaj* is used to indicate "spouses." See Wadud, *Qur'an and Woman,* 17–20.

30. See Hibba Abugideiri, "Allegorical Gender: The Figure of Eve Revisited," *American Journal of Islamic Social Sciences* 13, no. 4 (Winter 1996). This article discusses the narrative of creation as understood by traditional Muslim exegetes and found in oft-cited hadith commentary in order to show how Wadud's hermeneutical model yields a gender-balanced reading of this allegory, and of Eve in particular.

31. Ibid. Included as "genuine" were prophetic traditions approved by legal-theological consensus, with the result that the authenticated hadith came to contain strands of differing, sometimes even contradictory traditions that were preserved by their supporters' consensus. See Stowasser, "Gender Issues," 32. I argue in my article on Eve that the "crooked bone" hadith is one such tradition, for it clearly contradicts the Qur'an.

32. Abugideiri, "Allegorical Gender," 524, 526.

33. Wadud, *Qur'an and Woman,* xi.

34. Ibid., 2.

35. For a discussion of the different methodological approaches to the Qur'an from classical to contemporary times, see Stowasser, "Gender Issues."

36. Stowasser indicates that the aim stated here is meant to refer solely to medieval tafsir, while I understand it to mean the aim of the entire corpus of tafsir literature. Stowasser, "Gender Issues," 32, 38.

37. Ibid., 39.

38. Wadud, *Qur'an and Woman,* ix.

39. Ibid., x.

40. Stowasser, "Gender Issues," 39.

41. Syracuse, N.Y.: Syracuse University Press, 1996.

42. Among the goals presented by Sonbol in her introduction are: first, to focus on the history of women, family law, and divorce in order to assess gender relations and the status of women, not by focusing on ideology or discourse but on the historical specificities of different Muslim societies; second, to raise important questions about the history of women and the family that have received little attention in scholarship, such as issues of gender violence and laws pertaining to children and non-Muslim minorities; finally, to propose new methodolo-

gies and theories for understanding the history of women and the family. See Sonbol, *Women, the Family and Divorce Laws in Islamic History*, 14–18.

43. Ibid., 11.

44. See Sonbol, "Law and Gender Violence in Ottoman and Modern Egypt," in *Women, the Family and Divorce Laws in Islamic History*.

45. Amira El-Azhary Sonbol, "*Ta'ah* and Modern Legal Reform: A Rereading," *Islam and Christian-Muslim Relations* 9, no. 3 (1998): 293.

46. Amira El-Azhary Sonbol, "Rethinking Women and Islam," chap. 6, this volume.

47. With Wadud, a professor of religious studies, the emphasis is on the intention behind the text, actually on the hermeneutics of "reading" the Qur'anic text where the context provides the impetus for the necessity of such a reading. Sonbol, an historian, focuses on the historical context in order to assess how the religious text is applied.

48. Sonbol, "Introduction," 7.

49. Elizabeth Warnock Fernea, "Foreword," in Sonbol, *Women, the Family, and Divorce Laws in Islamic History*, x.

50. See Sonbol, "Rethinking Women and Islam."

51. Sharifa Alkhateeb, interview by author, Sterling, Virginia, April 18, 1999.

52. "The North American Council for Muslim Women" (pamphlet, n.p., n.d.).

53. Alkhateeb, personal interview.

54. Included in the survey were questions such as, "What is the proper behavior of Muslims during war?" (prompting this question were the rapes by Pakistani soldiers in Bangladesh); and, "Do you recognize that there is such a thing as marital rape in a Muslim marriage?"

55. To identify these women as "feminists," or even as "Islamic feminists"— a growing trend in women's studies on the Muslim world—obscures their contribution to religion as a whole. Indeed, the particular kind of gender jihad that they wage is not only against a Muslim androcentric orthodoxy, it is equally a struggle against what is essentially a racist secular ideology—that is, Western feminism. Instead, they attempt to create a legitimate Islamic female presence that requires no legitimation, by either an androcentric or a foreign discourse.

56. Elizabeth Warnock Fernea, *In Search of Islamic Feminism* (New York: Doubleday, 1998), 414.

57. See Ali A. Mazrui, "Islam in a More Conservative Western World," *American Journal of Islamic Social Sciences* 13, no. 2 (Summer 1996).

58. Amira Sonbol, private email message to Hibba Abugideiri, April 21, 1999.

59. Jane I. Smith, "Joining the Debate," *The World and I*, September 1997, 61.

60. Stowasser, "Gender Issues," 42.

61. Ibid., 30.

62. Ibid.

6

Rethinking Women and Islam

Amira El-Azhary Sonbol

A normative view of Muslim women is as victims of a patriarchal order defined by Islamic laws, traditions, and practices. According to this perception, while modern states allowed them to emerge from seclusion to participate in society through education and employment, history shackled them with deeply entrenched social habits that hold back reforms designed to allow women greater freedom and rights. In this conception of Muslim women's history, the past is painted as a grim picture of seclusion in harems, a dark period when women constituted property to be bartered in marriage and when their purity was guarded so as not to bring shame to their families. In short, the purpose of a Muslim woman's life was to bear children, uphold her family's name, and serve the man she was given to in marriage. She had little say in her life either before or after marriage, and once married, she could not separate even from an abusive husband.

This view is shared by many Western scholars through whose eyes the non-Muslim world has come to understand Islamic history and society. Muslim feminists who are actively involved in international organizations and Western feminist circles also share it. This group of scholars and activists, the majority of whom are women, depend largely on demographic and sociological studies about the status of women in the Islamic world today. They also make reference to the Qur'an and other sources of Islamic law, and they see Islamic law as an unchanging body of laws based on scripture and the interpretations of medieval *fuqaha'* (clergy).[1] They see the lives of Muslim women as dictated by medieval laws that have no place in a dynamic modern world that they identify with the West, where women have gained significant economic and political rights. They compare the favorable life of women in the West to the "servitude" of women in Third World countries in general, and Islamic countries in particular.

In defense of Islamic gender practices, some Muslim scholars have demonstrated how Islam actually improved the condition of women, who were much worse off before Islam. They point out that in pre-Islamic Arabia, women were controlled by their clans as property and suffered through female infanticide and polygamous marriages. The Qur'an gave women status equal to men in the eyes of God since both were expected to uphold the same moral standards and perform the same rituals of *shahadah* (declaration of faith), prayer, fasting during Ramadan, pilgrimage to Mecca, and *zakat* (almsgiving). Islam also gave women financial security since they received a dowry from their husbands at the time of marriage, *mut'ah* compensation (compensation when a marriage was ended against a wife's wishes, compensation for the enjoyment and benefits of the marriage that would be denied her), and a one-year alimony following divorce. Women also inherited property, and could invest their wealth in trade or any other profit-seeking activity. Islam also assured women proper treatment by their spouses and condemned abuses like wife beating or rape. Differences from what Islam prescribed in the application of gender laws by Islamic societies today are to be blamed on the interpretation of *fuqaha'* as well as traditions that predated Islam that were adopted into Islam. Interestingly, this group of scholars, like the critics of Islam, use scripture and *fiqh* almost literally, if for different ends.

Scholars who believe that women had greater freedom and rights before the coming of Islam represent a third point of view. They show that the issue of female infanticide has been exaggerated and that infanticide was practiced in a very limited way and only when clans were in dire need. Further, both girls and boys suffered from infanticide, although girls were considered more dispensable at times when tribal protection was a constant battle. It is true that the Qur'an guaranteed inheritance and dowry rights for women, but women inherited only half what men received, and the dowry was usually given to the father, and more often than not it never reached the hands of the bride. Furthermore, women of certain pre-Islamic Arabian tribes actually cohabited with several men among whom they chose the fathers of their children. They contracted their own marriages, did not wear a veil, rode into battle with their tribes, and were intellectual leaders, poets, and prophets. Islam as interpreted by fuqaha' established a patriarchal order that denied women the freedoms they enjoyed before Islam. This third group of scholars, mostly Muslim women but among whom are some male scholars, draw upon the Qur'an and fiqh but go beyond their literal meaning, reinterpreting the Qur'an and questioning the validity of the prophetic traditions. They study connections between Qur'anic verses (*ayas*) and discuss the historical context of each verse to determine the meaning and authenticity of traditions. Similar methods are applied to prophetic traditions and exegetic literature.

At first view, these depictions seem to contradict one another; they actually but represent different outlooks dependent on the ideology of the author and the particular sources used. One problem with all three approaches is that they use pre-Islamic Arabia and the life of Bedouin women as a "takeoff" point for the evolution of Islamic societies and as the social basis of gender. Tribal habits and traditions continue to form the model for social and gender relations even though Islam has expanded and developed and exists today in highly urbanized communities with direct impact on gender. It should be added that the views described above form a basis for reform efforts by governments, individuals, and Islamic groups—both liberal and fundamentalist. While Muslim women have been strongly involved in reassessing the history of women and the impact of Islam on their lives, very few have actually attempted a "woman's" interpretation of the Qur'an. Those who have, have done so cautiously, which accounts for their wide acceptance among Muslim thinkers, liberal and conservative alike. For example, Zaynab al-Ghazali is not only a recognized and respected thinker, she is widely acclaimed by conservative 'ulama'. So is 'Aisha 'Abdal-Rahman, better known as Bint al-Shati'. Her Qur'anic interpretations are widely respected, and her columns appear regularly in popular newspapers. Regarding the parts of the Qur'an that deal with gender relations, there is little difference between the interpretations of Bint al-Shati' and al-Ghazali and those of their male counterparts. The most radical departure is in al-Ghazali's conclusion of *Surat al-Nisa'* (4:3) that "one wife sufficed." Verse 4:3 is the Qur'anic verse that is used as the authority for a Muslim man to take as many as four wives (it will be the focus of part three of this paper). But al-Ghazali's discussion of 4:3 itself does not depart from the dominant male paradigm.

Women's lack of participation in Qur'anic interpretation should not be surprising, however, given the fact that Muslim theology has been almost exclusively a male pursuit. It is true that certain historical figures, like the Prophet Muhammad's wife 'Aisha, are seen as important transmitters of *hadith*. It is curious that a large number of commonly used hadiths establishing unequal gender relations are related back to the Prophet's wives, who have been granted intellectual authority by male exegetes. What better way to establish patriarchal gender relations than by emulating the Prophet's actions within his own household? Once such knowledge was established and accepted, there was little room to question it without appearing to be an immoral threat to the Islamic community. The problem is in the knowledge, the construction of this knowledge, and the history that has been established and widely dispersed by religious and political authorities. This is where questioning must begin, and it can only be done through intensive historical deconstruction based on the actual experience of Muslim communities. Here literature—poetry, chronicles, biographies—proves problematic since it, too, is interpretation. Like fiqh, it is a cultural product and hence a reflection of people's ideas, feelings, and struggles, their reactions to socioeconomic conditions and other complexities of human life. There is a great need to reconsider this literature as well as move toward more popular literature in the past and present. But it cannot be stressed enough that using literature or exegetics alone as a source to study gender has been the cause of great misunderstandings. The actual lives of women rather than commentaries on and interpretation of their lives have to be the focus for any future research agenda if the imagined history of Muslim women is to be deconstructed.

However contradictory this may sound, perhaps one should also caution that, even though women have not been participants in what may be termed official theological interpretation, they were nevertheless involved in defining social and gender relations and hence the legal principles applied in Islamic law and courts. The study of concrete social experience makes this fact almost indisputable even though fiqh dismisses it. While archival records reveal active social participation and legal awareness on the part of women, fiqh depicts Islamic patriarchy as crowned by an absolutist male while women are commanded and obedient, unseen and unheard. In short, women are imagined as victims and objects and not as active participants. Women's contribution to *ijtihad* belongs to everyday life, decision making, and conflict negotiation. It is there that norms and traditions are set, and it is in these norms and traditions that gender relations reside.

In the following discussion, I attempt an interpretation of certain important issues concerning gender established by the Qur'an. In so doing I realize that this is a woman's interpretation and will probably prove controversial. It is but one reading that takes into account historical context, fiqh interpretation in the past and present, laws practiced in Islamic countries today, and the application of gender laws in shari'ah courts before the modernization of laws in the nineteenth and twentieth centuries as well as in reformed courts. For the purpose of specific court evidence, I use records from Egyptian Ottoman and modern courts the subject of which has been of special interest to me in my career as researcher. Following a short interpretation of the history of women as seen through these records, I do two things. First is a general interpretation of gender in the Qur'an with an emphasis on equality and what has been popularly called "the rights of women," although the Qur'an does not deal with human rights as much as God's rights. It is in Islam's vision of human equality that human rights can be understood. Second, I take one of the most controversial issues in Islam, polygamy, and discuss the history of its interpretation as well as give my own view of the issue. My conclusions show the interconnection between the various parts of this study and discuss the need for further research and rethinking.

Historical Background

Recent studies of the Ottoman period show that Muslim women, like women elsewhere, lived in patriarchal societies where it was usual for a male—husband, father, brother, or uncle—to head the household. Within this patriarchal order, women were expected to obey their husbands, men sometimes married more than one wife, and guardians had absolute power (*wilayat al-ijbar*) over their minor children—both boys and girls—whose marriages and divorces they arranged as they saw fit. A cursory look at archives may give the impression that divorce was the sole prerogative of men, that women could be incarcerated against their will by husbands, that physical abuse was common, and that Islamic law was applied with little change over the centuries. A closer reading of archival records, however, shows another dimension to this picture.

For one thing there are clear differences regarding the laws applied by shari'ah courts depending on place and time. Even though there was clear consistency in the application of law by judges, there are significant differences depending on the particular *madhhab* (school of law) being applied, the nature of society—whether urban or rural, tribal or peasant—and the age. Furthermore, various fuqaha' of the same *madhhab* interpreted the law differently. So the idea that Islamic law is unchanging is clearly based on an incomplete reading of *fiqh* without reference to actual legal practice as presented by court records, a common problem concerning the use of Islamic sources. It should be added that court records themselves are problematic since they differ greatly in quality and quantity from one part of the Islamic world to another, and even the most abundant and detailed records (Egypt, Turkey, Syria, and Palestine) do not tell the whole story. Nevertheless, archives supplemented by literature, biographies, and *fatawa* (legal opinions rendered by a recognized religious authority) of the particular decades under investigation give us a pretty good picture of life in Muslim societies.

The modern period in the Islamic world is generally dated as beginning with the nineteenth century, following Western chronologies based on the experience of the West. Today, however, modernization paradigms structured on "takeoff" points are being replaced by others emphasizing historical continuities. As more historians trained in local languages began deconstructing the normative exotic and passive picture of Muslim societies, women's history became both the beneficiary and an important reason for this development. Thus, it is clear that the lives of women throughout most of the nineteenth century continued much as they had in the eighteenth, and that the reforms experienced by women at the hands of nation-states had mixed results. Legal reforms continued at different paces throughout the nineteenth and twentieth centuries, depending on the particular Muslim country. Egypt and Turkey seem to have been the pioneers in this area, even though other countries—like Lebanon and Tunisia, which banned polygamy—have caught up and extended rights to women exceeding those given to them in Egypt. Meanwhile, Turkey is experiencing a revival of Islamic traditions after a long period of secular government following World War I.

Modern legal reforms introduced a multi-tiered system that created what became known as "personal status law." Without doubt, new state laws and reforms gave women access to greater public services in such areas as education and health. This was part of government mobilization efforts involving centralization, administrative rationalization, bureaucratic growth, industrialization, and westernization. Political rights were also extended to women, and they were given relative job equality with men. Laws and legal procedures supposedly applied equally to both. But if equality was the intent, as is proclaimed in the various constitutions and national charters of Muslim countries, in practice women experienced a marked deterioration in gender relations under what can only be called state patriarchy since the government extended its authority over all matters of family, gender, and personal relations.

Through committees formed to compile new laws and legal procedures, the right of women to divorce became minimal while the rights of men to divorce their wives at will and to marry more than one wife were upheld and extended. New laws based only superficially and selectively on the Islamic *shari'ah* established systems and institutions that allowed for the forcible incarceration of women by their husbands. Known in Egypt as *bayt al-ta'ah* (house of obedience) and in Tunis as *dar al-ajwad* (house of notables), these structures coerced women to do what their husbands wished (or their husbands and fathers, in the case of dar al-ajwad).[2] Courts committed women to these institutions of incarceration, and the police were used to deliver them to husbands and fathers against their will. While *ta'ah* (obedience) in Islamic law is reciprocated by the husband's responsibility for *nafaqah* (financial support), it never included forced incarceration of women. Shari'ah court records from before the time of the Ottoman empire and until the modern period show clearly that such an institution as bayt al-ta'ah did not exist and that wives had no trouble receiving a judgment of divorce. To be secluded at home unable to go out without a husband's approval was a choice left to the wife, and she could break it at will if she no longer wished to live with him.[3]

One of the most serious errors applied to the history of women concerns the concept of public/private spheres. In this view, the public was the sphere of men: here they practiced their professions, participated in politics, and formed the active part of society. The woman's domain was the home. There she was secluded and could not leave without being veiled and only if her husband permitted her to go out. It was only with modernity—and in the case of non-Western women, the coming of Western influences—that the strict divides between private and public life begin to blur. This understanding is at the heart of conservative efforts to veil women in the Islamic world today, to deny them work in the public sphere, and to confine their attention to the family. Qur'anic interpretation by conservative authors is directed to enforce segregation. Women's unveiling or leaving the private domain is seen as a Western innovation that needs to be rooted out of Islamic society.

Archival research proves that the private/public divide has questionable foundations in Islamic history. The more you read, the more alive the tableau of the premodern period becomes. If coming to court was a possible cause of immorality, as some medieval jurists wrote, then Islamic society must have been terribly corrupt. Women appeared in court routinely, daily. Every second or third entry in shari'ah court records involved women—women buying, selling, marrying, divorcing, reporting violence, demanding compensation or custody of their children, among other activities. This is in great contrast with the modern period, when mostly poor women who cannot afford the expenses of a lawyer come to court. Middle-class and wealthy women no longer make an appearance in court and instead are almost always represented by lawyers, brothers, fathers, or husbands. The accessibility of justice is one of the strongest virtues of the Ottoman period in comparison to the modern state, which codified the laws, centralized courthouses, and demanded representation by a lawyer class. The lack of participation by women in court procedures today and their delegation of such procedures to male relatives and lawyers are assumed to date from the premodern period, but this is not a true representation of the court culture of the time. One way we know this is that Ottoman courts required women to identify themselves. Some brought witnesses to vouch for their identity, but most were identified directly by the court clerks. In fact we often have the description of the woman standing in front of the court clerk in specific details.[4]

There is other evidence against the public/private divide, and here we should look at why women left the home in the first place. Given the number of court cases disputing the wife's constant leaving of the marital home for various purposes, one can conclude that it was natural for women to go out shopping, visiting, or to go to work. Husbands might dispute that and often withheld their *nafaqah*, as pointed out earlier. But that did not mean that women had to have their husbands' permission before going out. This is a fiction developed by modern thinkers who dismiss the pre-modern period and acclaim the benefits of modernity for women.[5]

The question of women's work is essential if we are to understand gender relations before the modern state came into being. Did women work? If so, what jobs did they perform? The picture regarding women and work is very interesting. Suraiya Faroqhi has shown that women in the Ottoman empire had an important role in silk manufacturing and weaving, although she mainly discusses secluded practices—that is, women not in a workplace but rather involved in a takeout system by which they produced their product at home. Interestingly, according to Faroqhi, women did organize into pressure groups, showing labor awareness.[6]

Egyptian archives give us much the same picture as Faroqhi—that is, women doing work at home and having access to the market in various ways to sell their product. We are also given detailed evidence of the retail aspects of women's activities. Whether this was a common practice in other parts of the Ottoman empire is worth exploring. The evidence suggests that it was very natural for women to be in the market-place, either to sell their goods or to shop. The evidence is in the form of court records dealing with disputes between husbands and wives be-cause of their constant shopping, or between men and women or women and women who dispute over business dealings. After all, the courts were a place to resolve disputes. The most common dispute has to do with physical brawling—two women beating each other up or several women ganging up on one of them. Often it is a man who is beating up a woman over strategic selling spots in the marketplace. In court it was normal for each to declare that that spot in the market was theirs and that the other had encroached upon it.

Other common cases of women quarreling in the marketplace in-volved charges of forced miscarriage, which if proven brought heavy compensation. The complaint was brought to the court as a financial dispute. Sometimes the claim was that another woman caused the quar-rel and that the miscarriage took place, but often a man is singled out as having caused the miscarriage. He is charged with beating up the preg-nant woman on purpose, perhaps because his wife had instigated a ven-detta or because the injured woman had encroached on his spot in the marketplace. This raises questions about the seclusion of women if strange men can actually beat them and cause them to miscarry! Records also show that women owned shops and property. As Afaf Marsot dem-onstrated, they also held *waqfs* (religious endowments) and were often assigned as executors of the *waqfs* and the estates of deceased relatives inherited by their children and siblings.[7] As executors they were respon-sible for the collection of income; and even when this job was delegated, it involved contact with strangers, including men. We also have direct evidence that women were running their shops themselves, although they might delegate this function if the shop was far away. This was the case with the Maghribi community of Alexandria, whose women inher-ited property in Tunisia or Morocco and delegated the collection of in-come to others—usually men, probably because they traveled and could carry the money back.[8]

In short, many of the assumptions of modern scholars and fuqaha' regarding the history of Muslim women are not founded on reality. Yet these assumptions continue to influence the way in which the Qur'an, like other sacred scriptures, has been used to build hegemonic patriar-chal discourses. Beliefs about the seclusion of women, women's work as private and in the home, veiling, men's responsibility as moral guides to wives as part of their *qiwamah* (leadership), men's right to divorce women at will while women's access to divorce is restricted, and polygamy are all central to these discourses. Constructed discourses gain a life of their own and become a reality having little to do with the original laws they supposedly represent.

Islam, like other religions, concerns itself with the role of women and men within society. The holy books of Jews, Christians, and Muslims contain basic principles, laws, and moral judgments concerning a woman's life and the conduct expected of her. Each generation of women has to cope with these fundamentals and tries to apply them to the particulars of life during their specific era. With the passage of time, each generation has also had to contend with the interpretations of these fundamentals by the previous ages. By the twentieth century, women had become bound not only by the laws ordained by scripture but also by their societies' understandings of the past. The experiences accumulated over centuries reflect diverse circumstances, economic structures, divisions of labor, political systems, and even international relations. Yet these experiences and their interpretation in modern terms are used to provide models for contemporary conduct.

Notwithstanding the fact that every society faced unique circumstances in its own time, and perhaps because each generation has seen its own practices as ultimately grounded in scripture, it has become customary to regard the interpretations of the religious scholars of the past as synonymous with God's intent expressed through holy books. Possibly, it is the lack of contemporary leadership matching what the "imagined" as a higher moral standard of the old standards of knowledge and piety that makes people today look to the past for guidance, or maybe it is simple nostalgia for a past world that is easier to understand now that it has gone. The most serious problem with this projection to the past is that the focus for interpreting the life of women in the modern world has been the early period of Islam. The *salaf* (forebears, forefathers) constitute the basic model, but this model is studied through the prism of the interpretation of fuqaha' throughout Islamic history as each addressed the problems of each successive age. The model of the salaf is therefore nothing but a construct of the succeeding generations; it represents the image rather than the concrete realities of life that modern women are supposed to live by today.

That Muslim theologians and scholars were reacting to the problems of their age and presenting their solutions to what they considered immoral or wrong—very much as they do today—has been lost to those demanding the application of models from early Islam without much concern for real research in the historical context. A good metaphor would be the sermons preached by modern popular preachers such as

Shaykhs Kishk or Sha'rawi of Egypt. From their continuous harangue regarding morality one would imagine that Egyptian society today is very immoral and corrupt, the women loose and the men unable to control their lusts. Needless to say, that is hardly the case. Egyptian society is quite conservative and pious, notwithstanding the moralist discourse. The modern period, like other historical epochs, needs to be studied from within its own historical reality. Cultural production is important to show us conflicting discourses and ongoing class struggle, but it must be seen as a cultural representation rather than concrete reality. The cases dealt with by the *muftis*, or Friday preachers, should also be seen for what they are: as dealing with specific problems, and representing a moral discourse of particular individuals with their own class and cultural baggage, rather than a general picture of Egyptian society.

In this modern age, Muslim women have experienced great changes. They have seen their societies modernize, industrialize, and interact within an increasingly smaller world in which no nation or society can stand isolated from the rest. They have been trying to come to grips with their changing roles while holding on to the fundamental laws presented by the Qur'an. Women, like men, have had to deal with a more aggressive existence, in which they increasingly share in the burden of supporting a nation. Islamic countries as a whole have had to deal with the modern age, the rise of nation states, capitalist or socialist transformations, change in family structure, and new methods and forms of education. All this has affected the male members of the community no less than the female, but, as in most social transformations involving male-dominated traditional societies, it is the changes in the rights and duties of women that have proven to be most controversial.

During the early years of the twentieth century, Muslim women experienced periods in which society encouraged their education, their public role, and a more liberal interpretation of religious laws. Those were times of revolutionary enthusiasm, in which state building was still an optimistic endeavor. During the last decades the reverse proved true. With the growth of political and economic difficulties, Muslim societies, faced with the frustrations of development and economic dependency, tried to compensate with a more puritanical approach to social and religious issues. In a way, this was an effort to control their communities' destiny in some fashion. One of the results has been a reorientation toward a stricter interpretation of the role of women and the whittling down of rights they had already won. At the same time, the maneuverability they had experienced in personal and family relations before the modern period was lost to them under the guise of reform.

The subject of Islam and women's rights has been part of an ongoing dialogue regarding the interpretation of the shari'ah since the end of the nineteenth century, when the impact of westernization began to bring about deep structural changes in various Muslim countries. One group of intellectuals and theologians has argued that to meet the challenge of modern times, their communities must become revitalized through a reopening of the door of ijtihad (interpretation). Through ijtihad, Islamic societies could hold on to the fundamentals of Islam while at the same time allowing for the transformations required by changing times. A second group, while not disagreeing about the need for ijtihad, has used sources of Islamic law to apply a more conservative interpretation and has looked to the past for ways to meet the challenges of modernization. Rather than try to mold Islam to changing conditions, they wish to mold modern Islamic society to Islamic law as interpreted by past generations.

Initiated during the period of *tanwir* (enlightenment), as some have referred to the late decades of the nineteenth century, this debate is taking an increasingly conservative direction today. While the first, more liberal group was more influential in the past,[9] with the increasing political, economic, and social problems of the last two decades, more conservative groups have gained in prestige and influence. Those who favor the more liberal argument have also turned more conservative, giving a stricter meaning to the Qur'an when it comes to the issue of gender. So even though there are clear differences between the liberals and conservatives in regard to political or economic issues, both have favored more patriarchal interpretations of Islamic laws dealing with what is termed the "woman problem."

Here I take particular issue with assumptions that it is Islam, as a religion based on a God-given law, that has held Muslim women back from gaining some measure of social and legal equality. As explained earlier in this article, such an approach undermines history by seeing Islamic law as an unchanging code and Islamic societies as stagnant waiting for a grand mover to enforce transformations. Like all other human societies, that of Islam has changed and transformed with time, changed technology, and circumstances. The laws applied, if based on particular codes, have in fact developed and mutated according to needs. Conservative methodologies applied today are creating rigid interpretations of the Qur'an that need to be addressed. The ijtihad applied here is an effort toward that end, so that the debate could be widened to include other points of view than the liberal and conservative perspectives that have dominated the discourse. It particularly emphasizes the need for women to be involved in rereading and interpreting fundamental laws set by the Qur'an. It is my belief that by looking to the Salaf for answers, one of the most important characteristics of Islam is being undermined: its flexibility. As any cleric will tell you, Islam is a universal religion and is meant to fit all places and all times. Today, the call for a return to Islam has taken upon itself a strict interpretation of the past and sees that reform of today's community should be based exclusively on the actions of those who came before. These actions are presented through the ideas of jurists rather than through the actual practice of society. Thus, whereas *turath* (heritage) literature fills the bookstores and libraries of Muslim thinkers today, little importance is given to research detailing the actual practices and application of laws, which jurists commented on or reacted to. In short, textual discourses are given greater validity than actual legal practices, and the texts selected and presented give an eternal, unchanging appearance to Islamic law fitting with modern state patriarchy.

Unfortunately, this prevailing methodology, while allowing for patriarchal hegemony, also denies the very universality of Islam so central to its message. After all, what is advocated is not a religion meant to fit all times and places but a selective reading from the accumulated interpretations of past clerics that fit the beliefs of conservative individuals and groups. Those who follow this path could be called fundamentalists but with qualifications, since they do not build their interpretations on a strict reading of the Qur'an alone; that would be counterproductive for their purposes. Rather, when it comes to controversial issues, they generally prefer to support their arguments by selected juristic interpretations from present and previous generations of *'ulama'*.

The issue of how Islamic law is to be interpreted is a vital one, not only for women's rights but because the methodology decided upon by the community will be of critical importance to the future of Islam itself. Those who hold on to the past as a way of holding on to Islam not only detract from the fundamental character of Islam as a universal religion, but also hold back their countries from advancing and developing in a world community quite different from that of the Middle Ages in which fiqh was formulated. Today various countries are considering whether to make the shari'ah the main law of the state, to adopt a combination of religious law and secular law, or to stick solely to secular law. It is my belief that if by shari'ah is meant the type of interpretation embraced by conservative groups, then such laws can only have a negative effect on the community. But if, as the great nineteenth-century Egyptian reformer Shaykh Muhammad 'Abduh advocated, we reopen the door of ijtihad and allow for a rereading of the Qur'an in terms of present-day conditions, the universality of Islam can be protected. Such a methodology could also prove to be a bridge between upholding the principles of Islam and at the same time allowing Islamic society to participate in the progress of world civilization.

Women and Gender Equality

> I have continued to stress to people the importance of [religious] knowledge, since it is the light by which one should be guided. But I have found that women are in greater need of being reminded of this than men, because of their disregard for knowledge, and their natural inclination and fascination for frivolous pleasures. Usually, a young girl is brought up at home and is not taught the Qur'an and does not know ablutions . . . and is never told about the rights of a husband before her marriage . . . perhaps she has seen her mother take from [her] husband's funds without his permission, and practice witchcraft on him, claiming legitimacy for this [action] as being aimed at winning his love. . . . [Furthermore] she prays while seated even though she has the ability to stand up, and intrigues to end a pregnancy [when it happens].[10]

Such a negative view of women by medieval scholars is publicized through reprints by conservative presses today to paint an image of women as being essentially sinful and lacking control over their own emotions, therefore society has to legislate controls on women's activities. In order to support his religious arguments about women, Ibn al-Jawzi used mostly hadith and fiqh in preference to the Qur'an. An example of this is his assertion that it is best for women not to be in the company of men, a view that has been used to justify the segregation of women and the restriction of their movements and associations. As proof he tells the following story: "As reported by Sa'id b. al-Musayyib, [who said] that 'Ali b. Abi Talib, peace be upon him, asked Fatima ['Ali's wife and the Prophet Muhammad's daughter], peace be upon her, 'What is best for women?' She answered, 'That they see not men and men not see them.' 'Ali continued, 'I informed the Prophet, God's prayers be with him, of this and he answered: 'Fatima is but a part of me.'"[11]

In the part of his work titled, "Warning Women against Leaving their Houses," Ibn al-Jawzi discusses why women should not leave the home and how they should dress if they have to. "A woman must not go out [of the home], for even if she [intended] no evil, the people would [still] not be safe from her. And if she is forced to go out, after taking her husband's permission, she should wear worn clothes . . . and make sure that her voice is not heard, and that she walks at the side of the road and not in the middle of it." As Islamic evidence for the above, he quotes a hadith of the Prophet, which he is using out of context: "'Aisha [the Prophet's wife], peace be upon her, said: I heard the Prophet of God, peace be with him, saying: 'Any woman who removes her clothes in other than her own home will destroy all that (love) that is between her and God.'"[12] What has one to do with the other is not clear, but this is often the case with such rules regarding women.

Based on this type of hadith methodology, fundamentalists are today constructing a moral hierarchy for gender. Little effort is made to compare the hadith with the Qur'an or to place the hadith within any particular context in which a conversation like this could have taken place. And given the fact that the Qur'an has no concept of "original sin," this picture of the essential sinfulness of women can have only a spurious basis. This is especially so given the general rules set up by the Qur'an that do not describe women as any more sinful by nature than men. Nor is Eve blamed for the fall, an idea that was imported into Islam from the Old and New Testaments. Actually, when the Qur'an discusses women and sin, it almost always discusses men and sin within the same discourse and uses a similar terminology. For example:

> "Say to the believing men that they should lower their gaze and guard their modesty, that will make for greater purity for them, and God is well-acquainted with all that they do, And say to the believing women that they should lower their gaze and guard their modesty, that they should not display their beauty and ornaments except what (usually) appears of them. (S. 24:30–31)

Unfortunately, even though the Qur'an recognizes both men and women as possible sinners, and, in fact, provides for equal punishment to both, we find that the burden of sin and shame has traditionally been put on the shoulders of women, who therefore must be secluded lest they cause evil. "Women are an 'awrah" (meaning a weak spot or genitals); the implication is then sexual weakness. "When she leaves [her home], she is accompanied by the devil." How can this image of woman as a walking 'awrah be reconciled with the above-quoted verse from the Qur'an? And why are women and not men burdened with potential sinfulness when the Qur'an speaks with equal terms about both? And does not the Qur'an not make gossip about another's immorality a serious sin, punishable with eighty lashes? 'Abd al-Mit'al al-Jabri of al-Azhar quotes Imam al-Ghazali in another misogynist hadith: "A woman is closer to her God if she is in a hollow cavity in her house, her prayer in the courtyard of her home is better than her prayer in the mosque, and her prayer inside her house is better than her prayer in her courtyard, and her prayer in her bedroom is better than her prayer in her house."[13] In short, various levels of purity are laid out, with the more secluded posited as the best. Does this not undermine the importance of communal prayers in Islam? If women cannot pray in a mosque with men, would it not be best for them to hold their own communal prayers, whose importance is emphasized in the Qur'an? Why presuppose sin in women given the Qur'an's admonishment not to presume slander, as S. 24:23 commands: "Those who slander unwary believing chaste women are cursed in this life and in the hereafter, for them is a grievous retribution."

Perhaps the most important contradiction in Qur'anic interpretation today in regard to sin has to do with stoning as a punishment for fornication. While today stoning is used to punish women for *zina* (adultery), and adultery has been made equal to flirtation and dressing-code violations in stoning cases in countries like Pakistan and Iran, there is no mention of stoning in the Qur'an. Rather, the punishment for zina is spelled out: "The adulteress and the adulterer, each receives a hundred lashes" (S. 24:2). As a legal basis for stoning, versions of traditions have been used that claim the Prophet's acquiescence to stoning for Muslims. Even though the books of fiqh do not lend much credibility to these, advocates of stoning for zina today expand on the prophetic story and give particular importance to a story that 'Ali b. Abi-Talib ordered stoning for fornication. Here again traditions of questionable validity are used in preference to the Qur'an, which is very specific about the punishment for zina and only accepts that such punishment—lash or exile, depending on the marital condition of the perpetrators—be exacted after a voluntary confession is rendered numerous times. A good example of a hadith that has been used for various purposes, the story being changed where suitable, has to do with the trip of the Prophet to heaven, *Isra'* and *Mi'raj*. The hadith is purported to go as follows: as the Prophet ascended to heaven with Gabriel, he saw women hanging from their breasts screaming. He asked Gabriel why they were being punished. The traditions that record Gabriel's answer mention women who foisted their bastard children on their husbands and women who committed zina. The connection between the two possibilities is obvious. It is not clear, however, why only women were being punished in hell for zina. What about the men with whom they committed zina? Can a woman commit zina and have bastard children without men? Either the hadith has little legitimacy, or it has been turned around and given a misogynistic interpretation. Interestingly, this story is often repeated by groups advocating stoning today. Besides, stoning must end in death, so what are we to do about the Qur'an's admonition that a *zani* (adulterer) be married to a *zaniyya* (adulteress), and not to a non-adulterer? ("An adulterer may only marry an adulteress or a non-believer and adulteress may only marry an adulterer or a non-believer" [S. 24:3].) How are we to justify such an *ayah* if fornicators—who are caught in the act, the act is proven, and they voluntarily confess several times—can still be married after they are punished? Clearly the punishment did not include death by stoning or any other means.

Furthermore, why is it that today in Iran and Pakistan women have been stoned while men are not, when clearly women cannot fornicate alone? One must conclude that such legal interpretations are based on gender bias and misogyny, the shari'ah being manipulated to justify such actions. Thus the possibility of man being the cause of or being capable of sin is given only lip service, while it is the woman who is treated as a being from whom the world needs to be protected.

Perhaps the most central theme in Islam is its emphasis on the well-being of the community, in its concrete form rather than the idealized Islamic community at large. The various rituals, dogmas, and moral precepts presented by Islam are intended to assure the cohesion of the community. Praying, fasting, pilgrimage, and paying the *zakat* to support the needy and the community's various projects are all meant to bring people together, to mold the community into a cohesive whole that stands collectively, a unity that completes and complements its various components. For unity to exist there must be equality, a theme central to the vision of Islam. The Qur'an tells us, "Mankind, fear God Who created you from a single soul, created from it its mate, and from then twain propagated countless men and women" (S. 4:1).

This vision of equality has been one of the mainsprings and central teachings of Islam. Today it is used to show Islam's sense of justice as race- and ethnicity-blind, not differentiating between one man and another, be one rich or poor, except in what is in their hearts. But this equality is not extended to women. Rather, the concept is given no more than lip-service and the numerous Qur'anic references to equality between man and woman are commonly disregarded, as the man is given a superior moral and physical role as guardian over his wife. Even scholars considered to be liberal have found ways to justify this inequality. For example, Fazlur Rahman discusses equality in the following terms:

It may, however, be pointed out that although woman, as a human being, occupies equal status with man and is treated as equal, and enjoys equal rights, privileges etc., the fact remains that there is a difference between the sexes. No amount of debating or discussion, physical exercise or hard industrial work can change her sex. As woman, her special function in life is different from that of a man and she is naturally equipped with a different physical, physiological, biological, and even psychological structure. Islam has taken these natural differences between the sexes into account in differentiating roles and allotting functions to each sex. Therefore to talk of absolute equality between men and women is complete nonsense.[14]

The judgment that total equality between men and women is "nonsense" (as Rahman puts it) is based on the biological differences between the two, and particularly on the fact that the woman is the one who bears children. But why should man have rights superior to those of woman simply because God created each to fulfill different biological functions? Is man's essence his biological function, then? Is there nothing that differentiates him from other animals? And can the emphasis not be changed to recognize the balanced equality of roles rather than biological differences, particularly at a time when a revolution in biomedicine may put these biological roles into serious question? Already advancement in the technology of firearms and security has made a man's physical protection of women less important. The point I am trying to make is that while God certainly created men and women biologically different in order to perform particular biological roles, it is the male view of these roles that has decided actual masculine and feminine legal rights and duties in Islamic societies. It is the male view that made the male sex superior and decided that, however hard women tried, they could never achieve absolute equality with men. According to Fazlur Rahman, that notion "is complete nonsense." But why the presumption that women would want to be men, just because they exercise to strengthen their bodies? Why would women want to change their sex or become male, except in a misogynistic view? If fundamental Qur'anic laws do not change, our interpretations of them can and should. This is what makes any holy book universal, applicable to all times and places, as every Muslim will tell you.

Were we to divide the laws and requirements of the Qur'an into the two categories of *ibadat* and *mu'amalat* (rituals and social relations), we would find that both women and men are required to follow the same moral code. Articles of the faith are the same for both, as are the various rituals of prayer, fasting, pilgrimage, tithing, and profession of faith—all are required equally of women and men.

> Muslim men and women, believing men and believing women, humble men and humble women, truthful men and truthful women, patient men and patient women, pious men and pious women, men who give to charity and women who give to charity, men who fast and women who fast, men who guard their chastity and women who guard [their chastity], men who mention God's name frequently and women who mention God's name frequently, for them has God prepared forgiveness and great reward. (S. 23:35)

In the area of mu'amalat (social relations), there is the same basic equality that requires every individual to place the well-being of the family and community foremost in his or her mind. Because of differences in the physical nature of men and women, as well as in the needs of society, special roles are assigned to each. However, these roles are equal in importance, with exact rewards for fulfilling, and punishments for not fulfilling, the duties allotted. Notwithstanding this evidence, the fact that different roles are assigned to men and women has, unfortunately, been used as a basis for perpetuating a male-dominated society, in which legal equality has been forgotten. Therefore, to assign a position of total dependence to women, and of legal dominance and guardianship to men over women, as is the rule in the Muslim world today, is not in accordance with the very foundations of Islam as presented by God's revelation in the Qur'an.

Perhaps one of the most controversial chapters in the Qur'an is Surat al-Nisa' 4, which states "Men are the protectors and maintainers of women." The Arabic original for "protectors and maintainers" is *qawwamun*, which has been understood to mean different things by different people. *Qawwam* is also explained as "Men are placed in charge of women" because God has endowed them with the necessary qualities.[15] Being placed in charge makes men the guardians of women, entrusts them with watching over the women's actions, and makes them the final arbiters of their fate. Other interpretations are more strict, making men liable for punishment for their wives' sins and thereby giving them the right to enforce their own view of morality upon the women they marry or for whom they act as guardians. Such interpretations have explained this phrase as meaning, "Men are pre-eminent over women," which gives them absolute power over them. Fundamentalists who support this interpretation argue that this Qur'anic verse gives the man the right to prohibit his wife from acting in any way he judges to be unfit, lest he pay the price for her sins. However, it is not clear how such an interpretation can be reconciled with a belief in *Mi'ad* (Day of Judgment), when each individual will have to answer for his or her own deeds and thoughts. Where does the responsibility of one individual for another's actions begin or end in a system in which salvation depends on individual piety and faith?

Since the following verses may hold the key to its true meaning, it is unfortunate that its first part is usually used alone:

> Men are the protectors and maintainers of women, because God has given the one more [strength] than the other, and because they support them from their means * Therefore the righteous women are devoutly obedient [*qanitat*, pious, obedient to God],[16] and guard in [the husband's] absence what God would have them guard.

This verse has been interpreted in many ways. In fact, it is a good example of the flexibility of Islam, which is malleable and able to suit various periods of time. This is important because it outlines a very basic pattern in the system of mu'amalat set out by Islam. What it does is discuss shared obligations—that is to say, it is a balanced verse. If we analyze it and try to understand it in its totality, what we get is the following: Men are responsible for protecting women from bodily harm, and providing food and shelter for them. Women, in turn, must remain faithful to their husbands, physically, emotionally, and materially. If not, then a number of punishments ensue.

But this balance is forgotten, and qiwamah is taken to an extreme. According to Ibn al-Jawzi, for example, "A woman must know that she is like a slave to the husband. She is not to do anything or spend of his money without his permission, must promote his good before her own or the good of her family, and must be ready to give him pleasure. She should [also] not flaunt her beauty to him, or mention to him any of his faults. . . . A woman must be patient in answer to her husband's cruelty the same as the slave is patient."[17]

Is the person here a wife or a slave? Perhaps the difference was not clear in the minds of those who interpreted the Qur'anic verse on qiwwamah in this manner. Why such ideas should be common today, should be widely publicized and made accessible to the Muslim public, is open to question, for certainly civil law forbids slavery and even Islamic laws shun it. One popular but questionable tradition attributed to the Prophet and used to support such arguments is, "If I were to order anyone to prostrate himself to another, I would have ordered the woman to prostrate to her husband."[18] How could this statement, however hypothetical, be reconciled with the basic Islamic belief that prostration is only to God, and that there is no God but God, the concept of *tawhid*, or unity, which is the very basis of Islam?

If Surat al-Nisa' tells us one thing, it is that the Qur'an calls for a division of labor between men and women within the sanctity of marriage. This becomes acceptable to both when they enter into a marriage contract. A man provides for the family's economic support. A woman who bears children is expected to educate them and to keep the home as well as the sanctity of the marriage. She owes her husband allegiance, but it is questionable that this means loss of her self-identity and individuality. She is expected to make the marriage work, to try to live peacefully without problems, and the same is required of the husband. Hence, marriage was meant to be a contractual relationship, one entered into willingly by two equal partners. Certain articles and agreements are stipulated in that contract, including the exchange of money and the right of divorce, which could be either the man's or the woman's. If one party does not fulfill the obligations of a contract, it becomes null and void, and the other party then has the right either to accept the new conditions or to terminate the marriage. Theoretically, the system as presented by the Qur'an is one of impartiality to either of the sexes; it is meant to assure the strength of the foundation of the marriage, and hence the community. Each party assumes certain obligations and must fulfill a role, not to be broken by either side while keeping the other bound.

This interpretation is supported by other details from the Qur'an, such as the requirement that a woman must freely consent to the particular husband chosen for her, and that she should not be coerced into marriage any more than a man should. This matter was not questioned before modern times, since customarily the arrangement of marriages in traditional societies was the prerogative of the family, which made the choice of a mate for either a son or a daughter, who usually accepted its decision. Such a practice can easily be changed to suit modern times, since there is nothing in the Qur'an that says that the young people cannot choose their own mate. What the Qur'an does say is that the two parties in any marriage must consent, and that it is best for the woman to marry within the same social and economic class to which her family belongs. Therefore, in today's more open society, in which women play a more active economic, political, and social role, new interpretations can be applied so as to make the actual choice of a mate by either son or daughter as acceptable as one made by the family.

Another very important verse in the Qur'an, which indicates the significance of considering marriage as a contract based on equality between the two partners, talks about who holds the *'ismah,* or bond, of marriage—that is, the matrimonial authority. The decision on who holds this authority is specified at the time of signing of the marriage contract and is generally based on the agreement of the couple, taking into consideration class, wealth, or power. In a long discourse about marriage and divorce, which seems to be directed to men—even though, as indicated before, when the Qur'an talks to men it often addresses the community at large—the Qur'an at one point tells us:

> And if you divorce them before [the marriage is consummated] but after establishing their dowry, then [they are to receive] half the established dowry unless they waived it or it is waived by whoever holds in his hand the marriage knot. (S.3:237)

The Qur'an may talk about the "one in whose hands is the marriage tie" (italicized above), but even when women are given the 'ismah, in practice men continue to have the right to divorce them. So here, too, the Qur'an is interpreted in favor of the male.

The whole question of divorce in Islam is open to interpretation. Generally speaking divorce has been made the right of men, who, unless the right is given to women at the time of marriage, have full prerogative to implement divorce procedures. The general explanation for this imbalance refers to the differences in the male and female temperaments: women are more likely to become angry and act in haste, after which they regret their actions, while men tend to be more restrained and circumspect. This, of course, is questionable, and shows a male-centered view of relations between the sexes. The important thing is that it is not supported by the Qur'an, in which, when it comes to divorce, there is the same principle of equality that is meant to guide male-female relations in other matters. Surat al-Nisa' indicates that if a wife fears that her husband may desert her, or if he shows hostility toward her, then she has sufficient cause for alarm (allowing her to question the validity of the marriage). The Qur'an does call for attempts to bring the two parties together, but recognizes that reconciliation may not be possible: "If they were to part [divorce], God will provide each from His abundance, for God is Generous, Wise" (S. 4:130). Therefore there is a realization that, notwithstanding who holds the marriage contract, women may have the basis for a divorce.

What is even more interesting about these provisions is the choice of the word *nushuz* in regard to men: "If a wife fears *nushuzan* [desertion] on her husband's part." The word *nushuzan* is defined as "violation of marital duties on the part of either husband or wife, specific recalcitrance of the woman toward her husband, and brutal treatment of the wife by the husband."[19] That is, what we have here is an equality of reasons leading to divorce. Unfortunately, the word "nushuz" today is used to describe a woman only; one hardly ever hears of a husband who is *nashiz*.

As for conduct within the marriage, what is expected of man is very similar to what is expected of woman: total fidelity to the partner and to the family. The Qur'an is very clear on the rights of the husband, the wife, and the children within the family. Women are not seen as being evil; it is their goodness that is stressed (S. 4:124–27). Men are admonished to treat them fairly, to honor them, to watch out for their economic and marital rights, which include the right to a sexually active marriage, and to give them respect, love, and affection. The man is given the right to marry one, two, three, or four women, but only if he is capable of treating them equally, a challenge the Qur'an recognizes as perhaps impossible to achieve. Since each individual is judged according to what is in his heart, more than by his deeds, it is almost impossible for a man to marry more than one woman and still be totally impartial among them, fulfilling his obligations to them equally as husband, friend, and lover. (This point will be expanded on later.)

Notwithstanding all the evidence presented here, the usual characterization of the role of the male within the family is one of total superiority: he is the arbiter of the family's fate and the judge of his wife's actions. Since there has to be a leader in any group to prevent chaos from taking place and since man is the protector who shoulders the financial burden, he holds the reins of power. What can the woman hope for in such a marriage? The traditional answer is that the husband is expected to deal fairly with his wife, and that she must act in every way so as to assure that he will remain fair and faithful to her. In brief, the husband is the ruling member of the family, while the wife is a passive participant whose only role is to please her husband for fear of divorce, cruelty, his taking another wife, or neglecting her sexually and emotionally. The husband, it is true, is encouraged to listen to his wife's advice—the example of the Prophet being given—but he is not required to take such advice seriously; in fact, how could he take her advice seriously when she is but a passive, isolated member of their community?

Perhaps the problem is that the only role women are supposed to play is within marriage. This limitation, however, is not supported by the Qur'an, nor by the Sunna of the Prophet, whose first wife and the mother of his children, Khadija, was one of the great merchants of Mecca for whom the Prophet worked before their marriage. His young wife 'Aisha led armies in person against 'Ali bin Abi Talib, the Prophet's cousin and Islam's fourth caliph. It is, furthermore, not supported by Islamic history, in which women have played important roles in the economic life of their communities. The marriage contract requires that the man be responsible for all household expenses, including his wife's needs. The dowry that he pays to her father is to be given to her to use as she wills. She has the right to inherit and own property, whose control is to be kept in her own hands and not transferred to the husband at the time of marriage.

But while such rights are sanctioned by the Qur'an, we find that fundamentalists dispute them, preferring interpretations that favor the male even in today's family in which both husband and wife may work outside the home and provide it with financial support. Once more the Prophet is quoted: "A woman is not allowed to donate part of her wealth if the marriage contract is held by her husband, except with the permission of her husband."[20] The justification given is that the wife may be richer than the husband but that should not reduce his power over her. If such a hadith is to be proven to be authentic, it must first be reconciled with the Qur'an's admonition that a husband should be of the same economic status as his wife (kafa'ah). Furthermore, where the Qur'an speaks of the husband's role as regards his wife's wealth, it is to warn him from trying to cheat or rob her. Fazlur Rahman writes: "She keeps her property acquired before marriage and has no legal obligation to spend on her family out of her personal wealth. She is also entitled to a dowry (mahr) from her husband. She may invest her property in any way she likes or thinks best. She is quite independent, and even keeps her maiden name and does not merge it after marriage with her husband's, as happens in Western, African and Asian countries."[21]

There seems to be a clear guideline in the Qur'an to the effect that the woman is expected to contribute to her community. The wives of the Prophet, for example, were expected to do more than stay at home and play a passive role. Consider this passage in S. 33:28: "O Prophet! Say to your wives: if you desire the life of this world and its glitter, then come, I will provide for your enjoyment and set you free in a handsome manner." It is usual to consider this passage as referring to the need of women to spend more time in prayer, rather than a directive for them to take an active interest in their communities. But that cannot be so when one considers the active commercial role taken by the Prophet's first wife, Khadija, or that of his other wife, Zaynab b. Jahsh, who worked for the poor, "for whom she provided from the proceeds of her manual work, as she was skillful in leather work." Yusuf Ali's commentary on this verse supports my point: "But all the consorts in their high position had to work and assist as Mothers of the *Ummat*. Theirs were not idle lives, like those of odalisques, either for their own pleasure or the pleasure of their husband. They are told here that they had no place in the sacred Household if they merely wished for ease or worldly glitter."

Islam, like other religions, has had to deal with changing times. Today the Islamic world faces the challenge of a world that is being transformed at ever increasing rates. The question is whether Muslims will be able to hold on to their religion, traditions, and central belief in God while at the same time allowing their societies to develop along with the rest of the world. The question is not an academic one, since weakness means dependency, and the weakness of the Islamic community can only lead it to a position of subservience vis-à-vis the more developed nations. The experience of the last decades should have made this clear. Islam itself, as a religion, possesses the instruments of flexibility and universality, which cannot exist without human equality. It is up to Muslims today to use Islam in the way it was meant, to make God's commandments applicable to all time, rather than to try and hold back the hands of time.

Why Four Wives?

If you fear that you will not be able to deal justly with the orphans, marry women of your choice, double, triple, quadruple, but if you fear that you shall not be able to deal justly [treat them equally with justice?], then only one, or [she?] whom your right hands possess [hold?], that is best so you would not be unjust. (S. 4:3)

There is general agreement among Islamic thinkers that this ayah was received by the Prophet Muhammad following the battle of 'Uhud in which a large number of Muslim men were killed. Yet, notwithstanding this general agreement in regard to the specific context surrounding this ayah, it has been used as legal basis for permitting men to take up to four wives at any one time. As for the part of the ayah stipulating the condition that polygamous men must treat their wives equally, it is generally relegated to a man's accountability on the Day of Judgment. The logic in this contradictory interpretation—one part of the ayah being used for the here and now, while the second part is left to the hereafter—is a good example of the patriarchal interpretation of the Qur'an.

A number of issues pertaining to this verse are directly connected to the issues of marriage, divorce, and obedience discussed earlier. I will approach the matter from two particular points: first, the context and placement of the verse within the larger context of the Surah on women; and second, the particular number of four indicated.

The Context

As an introduction to Surat al-Nisa' in his translation of the Qur'an, Yusuf Ali explains that "the subject-matter [of the surah] deals with the social problems which the Muslim community had to face immediately after [the battle of] Uhud. While the particular occasion made the necessity urgent, the principles laid down have permanently governed Muslim Law and social practice." And so it has been. Answers to specific and temporary problems were made into universal laws.

While it is usual to take 4:3 as is, even disregarding all except the part that mentions four wives, it is only by considering the ayah from within the larger surah and its placement among other ayas, and analyzing its reasons of revelation (*asbab al-nuzul*), that we can begin to understand the significance of Qur'anic interpretation to gender laws in Islamic history and contemporary society. It is no exaggeration that while asbab al-nuzul seem to be very clear, the interpretation regarding the purpose behind the ayah has changed depending on historical context. While the number four remains constant, the legitimacy and justification for the number of wives has changed according to social pressures. Similarly, other important issues raised by Surat al-Nisa', clear when the Qur'anic text is read, change in interpretation given time and place.

To begin with, the particular context for S. 4:3 is supported by the general subject matter of Surat al-Nisa'. The context is also supported by pertinent prophetic traditions. Surat al-Nisa' begins with an admonition to humanity that they should fear God to whom they are accountable (S. 4:1). The surah then immediately moves to warn against robbing orphans or exchanging their property for less than its worth, and admonishes the hearer to give orphans the property that belongs to them (S. 4:2). Following on this theme of treating orphans fairly, Surat al-Nisa' then moves to discuss a very specific situation that is recorded in a prophetic hadith (S. 4:3):

> Ibrahim b. Musa related that Hisham informed him that Ibn
> Gurayh said that Hisham b. 'Urwa informed him that his father

said that 'Aisha *radiyya allahu 'anha* (God's mercy be upon her),
related that a man had an orphan [meaning was the guardian of
an orphan] and he married her (*nakahaha*). The orphan owned a
palm-grove which he withheld from her and he had no real affection for her [*lam yakkun laha min nafsihi shay'uin*]. The [Qur'anic]
lines *Awa in khuftum an la taqsitu fi al-yatama* (and if you fear that
you cannot treat orphans justly) were revealed because of him.[22]

If, as is always emphasized by fuqaha', prophetic traditions are the
key to understanding the meaning of the Qur'an, then the purpose of S.
4:3 is clear through this prophetic tradition. It is further confirmed by
another on the same subject—probably a version of the one quoted
above, and also referred back to 'Aisha.

[T]he orphan under guardianship of her *wali* (guardian) . . . he
covets her wealth and her beauty and so desired to marry her
without giving her the dowry of her equals. . . so they [guard-
ians] were forbidden from marrying them [orphans] except if
they would treat them justly.[23]

'Aisha continues in this tradition to compare the situation of a beautiful, wealthy orphan who is coveted by her guardian to the orphan who
is neither wealthy nor beautiful and therefore finds no one wanting her
for a wife. The comparison was meant to show that the guardian coveted the wealth and beauty of his ward while caring little for her. Hence,
S. 4:3 asks the guardians of orphans to leave them alone and look elsewhere for wives. This meaning is reconfirmed in expanded and yet similar terms in S. 4:127.

In short, the context of the verse is indisputable as is the admonition
to leave orphans alone and turn to other women for wives. Before discussing the number of wives mentioned in the verse, it is important to
ask why marry at all and how to go about choosing a wife or wives? The
first part of S. 4:3 only asks that men not deal unjustly with orphans and
that they look elsewhere for wives. The second part of the verse presents
alternatives to those men who may covet their wards, indicating that
they could take other wives from among those who please them. But
which women fit as possible other wives? While the second part of the
verse points to slave women as one possibility, we have to look elsewhere in Surat al-Nisa' and other chapters of the Qur'an for answers
about who are possible wives and why men should marry.

Surat al-Nisa' 4:25 gives us one indication regarding the choice of a
wife. "If any of you are [financially] incapable of marrying free believing

women, they may wed believing girls from among those whom your right hands possess." Yusuf ʿAli explains that the girls referred to by the verse are not slaves, that is, personal property: "[W]hat your right hands possess are 'captives' taken in a jihad. . . .Your right hands does not mean necessarily that she has been assigned to you, or is your property. All captures in war belong to the community. They are 'yours' in that sense."

This explanation makes more sense than the usual explanation that "what your right hands possess" are slave women—that is, the personal property of masters who can marry them. After all, if a man has enough wealth to own a slave woman, he probably has enough to marry a free woman. This explanation fits within the particular context of the time, when wars between tribes were the norm, as was the taking of women hostages from other tribes as *sabaya*. These hostages were normally owned by the tribe as a whole until ransomed or distributed as spoils to be treated as slaves, since their punishment is half that of a free woman (S. 4:25), but not born into slavery since they were captured in war.

In verse 36 of the same chapter, God speaks to men (meaning mankind, including both men and women), admonishing them to treat those around them well:

> Serve God and join not any partnered with Him; and do good to
> parents, kinsfolk, orphans, those in need, neighbors who are
> near, neighbors who are strangers, the companion by your side,
> the wayfarer, and what your right hands possess: for God loveth
> not the arrogant, the vainglorious.

The line "what your right hands possess" is popularly understood to mean slave women, which is indicative of the general acceptance that men have the power over women whom they marry or who are captives. However, since this verse is addressed to both men and women, the sense of responsibility toward other members of the community and toward "what your right hands possess" is in fact addressed to both men and women.

With time, however, "what your right hands possess" became defined as slave women, and the relationship between master and slave became defined as allowing sexual intercourse outside marriage, even when the slave woman was already married to another. How fiqh (juridical discourse) reached such conclusions is very telling about the connection between patriarchy, gender interpretation, and historical context. After all, S. 4:25 is clear in its declaration that it is best for "those among you who fear sin" (*al-ʿanat*, meaning zina or fornication) to take a wife. The rules against zina are very strict in the Qur'an, and nowhere is permission given for men to have sexual intercourse with women outside marriage, be they slaves or not. If anything, the Qur'an (S. 4:25) admonishes men to take slave women ('*ima*') as wives and not as concubines. Perhaps because the Qur'an does not forbid concubinage in so many words, it was considered permissible by later fuqaha' given the expansion of Islam, the taking of hostages, the lucrative commerce in slaves, and the concubinage habits of pre-Islamic society, which continued into the Islamic period. It is true that S. 4:24 includes "those your right hands possess" who may be already married in the category of women who can legitimately be taken as wives. But S. 4:24 discussed legitimacy for marriage and is clearly against lust: "thus has God ordained [prohibitions] against you except for these, all others are lawful, provided you seek [them in marriage] with gifts from your property, desiring chastity, not lust."

Furthermore, the use of "what your right hands possess" in this verse confirms that this refers to women captured in battle. It was the tradition among Arab tribes to consider the ties such women had with vanquished husbands as null and void, and hence their marriages dissolved by virtue of their capture by another tribe in war. So the verse points to that group. Even though the context and meaning are historically clear, the verse was read as allowing sexual relations with married slave women, notwithstanding that the verse is about marriage and is clear in its prohibition of sex outside of marriage. Here, a general rule was made out of a nonexistent rule. Since the Qur'an does not specifically forbid fornication with slave women, it became acceptable, even though the Qur'an encourages marriage to slave women and considers any form of sexual intercourse outside of marriage to be zina with clearly specified punishments.

A good example of this leap in interpretation is Malik b. Anas's explanation of "except those whom your right hands possess" as allowing "a man to wrench" (*yanza'*) his slave woman from her husband.[24] The method applied—that is, what is made into a general rule from what may not have been literally declared in the Qur'an—is not used throughout but rather where it serves patriarchy. In each case, the interpretation favors greater elite, patriarchal control, which must be expected given the fact that formal interpretation has been almost exclusively male and elite supported. Without doubt female interpretation would provide different methodologies. That is why we should look at fiqh as a formal male discourse rather than an expression of the true meaning of the Qur'an.

Surah 4:25 is also used to define marriage between Muslim men and non-Muslim women. Since the verse does not identify "women of the book" who are slaves as possible brides, fiqh does not include them in that category. The explanation of the verse given by the jurist Malik b. Anas is that Muslim men could marry free Jewish and Christian women but not Jewish and Christian slave women ('ima') (S. 4:32). The latter were then available to their masters as sexual partners outside of marriage. Here, a missing point was turned into a general rule, and then a further rule was added about which the verse had nothing to say—that is, that slave women of the book could legally be taken as concubines. According to Malik ibn Anas, "God made legal in his revelations the marriage of Muslim slave women ['ima'] and did not legalize the marriage of slave women of the Book, Jew or Christian . . . as for the Jewish slave or the Christian slave, she is legal to her owner by virtue of his ownership of her [bi milk al-yamin]. But a majussiyyah [Zoroastrian] slave woman is not legal to her owner [bi milk al-yamin]."[25]

Malik's interpretation is contradictory and problematic. If majussiyyah slave women may not legally be taken as concubines by their owners, then why may Muslim women legally be concubines? This is but one example of the methods used by different male interpreters, who find interpretations for existing legal practices and find Islamic legal precedent for them. By the time of Malik and the other schools of law, holding slave women by the wealthy was widely accepted, and buying slaves for sexual pleasure was also widespread. A reading of literature from the Umayyad and Abbasid periods confirms this. For example, the poetry of 'Amr ibn Rabi'a is full of adventures with beautiful women, many of whom were slaves. Then there is the extensive work of Isfahani, al-Aghani, which is a collection of stories of slave women, their exploits, their training, price in the slave market, and their love stories with customers and masters. It made sense that the fuqaha' and legists of the day would legislate for such privileges, which were often disputed in front of the qadi (judge), and that they would look to Islamic law for justification. Their interpretations should therefore be looked at in the context of their historical period rather than as a true representation of what the Qur'an was dealing with and the laws, specific and general, that God meant to establish for the Muslim community.

The Number Four

There is no question that S. 4:3 goes up to the number four in reference to wives. It is also clear that the verse was closely connected with a particular event; and given the details of the verse, it does not seem to have been meant to establish a general rule. Yet that is what it has become and how the words have been interpreted—as permission for men to take up to four wives at any one time. The interesting thing is that here the literal number is taken as an absolute number. Unlike other areas of interpretation, when assumptions are made without the existence of literal text, here a literal meaning is given to words taken out of context and without the rest of the verse being taken into account.

Perhaps most telling concerning the methodology followed in fiqh is the fact that when the question "why four?" is asked by the fuqaha', it is not to determine the validity of the number; that is taken for granted. Rather, the question is used rhetorically in an Aristotelian deductive formula in search of justification for an acknowledged truth. Some of these justifications are worth looking at for their ingenuity and to illustrate patriarchal efforts to make them acceptable to particular historical epochs and contexts.

In the most widely used justification, it is stated that the Qur'an limited the number of wives to four whereas men before Islam could marry as many wives as they wished. The number four is therefore seen as an improvement and benefit to women since now husbands are limited to only four. As pointed out earlier in this chapter, the question of whether Islam bettered the condition of women has long been a subject of debate. Without arguing this point here, it is enough to say that Muslims generally accept that Islam intended to improve the condition of women by limiting to four the number of wives that a man could have. But, one should ask, if bettering the condition of women was of particular importance to Islam, which recognized that reducing the number of wives improved the life of women, then why not limit the number to one wife at any one time?

Taking up the issue of number, the Moroccan Islamic thinker Muhammad Shahrour points to the similarities between the Qur'an's treatment of women and the issue of slavery. According to Shahrour, change was to take place slowly in both slavery and gender so as not to cause instability in human society. The direction change was to take, however, was clear from the beginning. That direction was toward less—less slavery and less polygamy, until with time both had ceased to exist, in fulfillment of the essential message of Islam: the equality of all in the eyes of God the Creator. However, Shahrour continues, while the fuqaha' did come to recognize the intent of the Qur'an to free slaves and put an end to slavery, they did not apply the same understanding to marrying more than one wife. The emancipation of slaves began with the Qur'an's admonishment to good Muslims that they use their money to buy and free them. This process continued into the modern world, when slavery was finally recognized as an evil system. Emancipation is often used as an example of the logic of the Qur'an, which fits the needs of each age and brings changes to humanity as people are able to comprehend and obey God's laws. When it comes to women, however, the same logic is not applied, and the rules pertaining to gender are seen as absolute. The Qur'an clearly sets the goal that only one wife should be allowed; and as Shahrour concludes, perhaps when men realize that they cannot treat several wives equally, then the evolutionary direction set by the Qur'an may finally become a reality.[26]

Shahrour is clearly opening important doors of Qur'anic interpretation that break new ground and employ a fresh methodology. However, neither Shahrour nor those who claim that Islam bettered the life of women really take up the question of "why four wives?" Why not five wives? Or ten wives, for that matter? The approach has been to justify the number four rather than to question the number. The method followed has been to make "four" a rational number based on actual human needs. Most common among these justifications is that a wife could be sick and unable to perform her wifely duties. While her husband could divorce her and marry another, that would not be fair to a wife who had done nothing wrong. Better that the husband should take a second wife while continuing to support the first, protecting her in his home and thereby honoring her rather than throwing her out without financial support and protection. What about taking a third wife? Here the most common justification has to do with a wife's infertility and a husband's wish to have children, particularly a male child. Even after science proved that it is the male's genes that determine the sex of the child, this justification continues to be voiced. Once more, marrying a third wife is justified on the basis that a husband should provide and protect a wife who cannot bear children rather than abandon her. It is even claimed that a son by one wife would enrich the marriage and be a consolation for the infertile wife.

Why a fourth wife? Among the usual reasons is that a husband could find himself attracted to another woman. In such a situation it is better that he contract marriage to her than commit zina, which can only threaten social morality. When issue is taken with this last reason—that a husband who loves one wife will surely not treat her equally with his other wives—it is always pointed out that the Prophet Muhammad preferred 'Aisha, but he made sure to spend each night with a different wife. The fact that all men are not the Prophet Muhammad is simply dismissed with statements that they should try to emulate Muhammad, that no one is perfect, and what is important is what is in their hearts. In short, it is a circular argument.

Other justifications for marrying four women include war and the deaths of men in war. Europe during the world wars is often cited as an example proving the superiority of Islamic gender laws: after all, large numbers of men killed in war meant that some women were left without husbands. Would it not have been better for European women to share a husband than not to have had one at all? To be denied sexual gratification, the solace of male companionship, and children are a worse punishment for women. During war, then, polygamy should become a duty for men to make up for the shortage of males. What about peacetime? Other arguments point to the need to propagate the faith, especially among Muslim communities who constitute minorities within larger majorities.

Interestingly, the views of women in this matter are considered something of a moot point. Since God ordained that men could have four wives, it is not up to women to decide otherwise. Even when the argument has to do with sexual gratification due to the lack of men, it is not up to women to agree that they need such gratification at the cost of sharing a husband with another woman. Again the argument is circular. In fact, an Egyptian law (Personal Status Law 44 for 1979) that tried to limit the number of wives by giving a first wife the right to a divorce if her husband married another, was strongly opposed in Egypt's Majlis al-Sha'b (People's Assembly) and reversed in 1980. The argument was that the law declared marrying a second wife constituted *darar* (harm) for the first wife, which allowed her to sue and receive a divorce since the shari'ah was clear about the right of a wife to divorce in case a marriage constituted darar to her. How could God ordain a darar and make it into law in the Qur'an? That was the argument raised by the male-dominated People's Assembly to reverse the laws: marrying a second wife could never constitute a darar since this was God's law. If jealousies arise between the two wives, then a husband will have to be lenient and treat them gently. In short, a wife had no recourse to divorce her husband because he decided to take a second wife unless she could prove that she suffered financial, physical, or mental harm other than that caused by the act of taking a second wife.

It should perhaps be pointed out that some contemporary conservative interpreters of the shari'ah contradict the way that the state has chosen to force a wife to stay with a husband who has taken a second wife. Thus, while applauding the Qur'anic law allowing for four wives as "a mercy" (*rahmah*) from God bestowed upon people and as a means of strengthening the Islamic *umma* through increasing its number which can be achieved best through "early marriage and polygamy,"[27] al-Sayyid Sabiq is very clear about the right of a woman or her *wali* (guardian or representative) to make a husband's monogamy a condition to be included in the marriage contract. He also considered the shari'ah as supporting the right of a woman to have her marriage annulled (*faskh*) if her husband took another wife.[28]

It is commonly believed that wives have always accepted husbands' right to take more than one wife, and that it is modernity and Western influence that have caused women to turn against such Islamic traditions. Having just one wife is therefore generally regarded as a Western import. As for divorce, Muslims see it as exclusively a male prerogative, so decreed by Islam. If women are demanding changes in marriage and divorce laws today, that too is regarded as foreign contamination to Islamic society. The two points are closely interrelated—that is, the right to have more than one wife whether a wife has agreed or not, and the right of a wife to separate from her husband because the marriage has caused her darar, or harm. Here is where archival research becomes of great service, and why, as stated earlier, dependence on shari'ah, fiqh, and fatawa, without going back to see how society actually enforced laws and moral codes, only serves to support the state patriarchy under which Islamic societies live today. Put simply, and as shown in the "Historical Background" section of this chapter, women have always found it objectionable that their husbands take second wives. Egyptian archives dating from the Ottoman period and continuing until the reform of laws and courts at the turn of the twentieth century give us concrete evidence to this fact. One of the conditions most commonly included by wives in marriage contracts was that the husband not take a second wife. If he did so, then he was considered in breach of contract and the wife had the choice to accept his action, to renegotiate the marriage contract, or to divorce, whereupon she had a right to all the financial commitments due her from her husband. It is interesting that it was common for husbands who found themselves in this situation to hide the fact that they had married a second time. If brought to court by their wives, they often lied about their second marriage, and the wives often had to bring evidence and witnesses for this second marriage. This is lucky for us since we get to know the details of marriages and contracts through such disputes. The point is that having more than one wife was neither widely practiced nor acceptable before the modern period or the advent of so-called Western "contamination."

As for divorce, it was not up to the qadi to force a wife to stay in a marriage against her will.[29] When she considered that she was suffering harm from a marriage, it was her prerogative to separate from her husband. This right existed whether it was a case of breach of contract or because of clearly defined shariʿah reasons, including incurable impotence, severe beatings, or lack of financial support. The right also existed when no such reasons existed. Even when a husband was "ideal" in all ways, the judge still had no right to force a woman to stay with him. In such a situation, she resorted to *khulʿ*, by which she surrendered all financial rights to the husband; and, if she was wealthy, she could also be expected to pay compensation because the breakup of the marriage was not due to any fault of the husband. Khulʿ was often negotiated between spouses: husbands often came to court with their wives for the purpose. However, unlike today, there is no indication that if a husband did not agree to khulʿ, or to be divorced from his wife, that he could force her to stay with him against her wishes. The significance of these details in regard to polygamy is obvious. They meant that if a man took a new wife, there was nothing to stop his first wife (or wives) from divorcing him. It should also be observed that having more than one wife was actually quite rare in Ottoman Egypt. If anything men—and women— seemed to marry, divorce, and remarry many times rather than marry more than one person at the same time.[30] Forcing a wife to stay with her husband against her will, limiting her ability to divorce, and narrowing the legal meaning of harm is new historically, quite modern, and has clearly been the prerogative of the nation-state. Selective use of Qurʾanic interpretation and religious exegetics has been the most important method for building up the new patriarchal order under which Muslim women live today. As mentioned earlier, S. 4:3 has been central to this discourse.

The example of the Prophet is always used to support the contention that men have the right to take multiple wives. This example is problematic because of the essentialist and final way it is presented: as an argument to end all arguments, for who can question the Prophet's actions? Yet the Prophet Muhammad's marital history is rather intriguing and can lead in a different direction. When he was married to Khadija, he never took another wife. Given her importance, which went beyond being his strongest supporter, she may not have been willing for him to take more than one wife. Later, when the Prophet had more than one wife, most actually asked him to marry them, and those whose marriage he contracted—like ʿAisha b. Abi Bakr, Hafsa b. ʿUmar b. al-Khattab, or Maryam al-Qibtiyya, who was given to him as a gift—accepted his taking other wives. In fact, the Prophet was known to divorce wives who were unwilling to remain married to him. This issue of choice is confirmed by Islamic law, which allows a girl whose marriage was contracted by her father while she was a minor to divorce a husband once she achieves maturity. (The same right is given to boys.) So a woman's choice to remain in or leave a marriage was always guaranteed by law. Ironically, this choice has been limited drastically by the modern state.

Stopping at the number four is convenient for accepting polygamy, but it could have another connotation altogether, one that involves accountability. The verse addresses a situation in which, due to the death of many at the battle of Uhud, the women and orphans left behind became wards of those who survived. As such, they risked having whatever property they had inherited or already owned appropriated by the new guardians, a situation clearly counter to the Qur'an, in which the rights of orphans constitute one central theme. So S. 4:3 can be seen as a statement by which the guardians are told that they have the power to marry as many of them as they want. After skipping "one," it goes on to "double," "triple," "quadruple." Why did it stop at quadruple? Why did it not begin with one? No explanation is given in the Qur'an; it simply goes on to indicate that if you fear you cannot treat them equally, then take only one (fa wahidah) or "ma malakat aymanakum," which is generally translated as "what your right hands possess" or "[a captive] that your right hands possess," as discussed above.

The first question to ask here is, why did S. 4:3 skip the number one? Secondly, why does it continue with the ordinals "double" (mathna), "triple" (thulath), and "quadruple" (ruba') rather than the cardinal numbers two, three, and four? If the intention was to specify a particular number, then the clearest reference would have been one, two, three, or four, or even to go directly to the maximum allowed number. But that is not how the Qur'an states the matter; rather, a multiple of one is presented. Why did it stop at ruba'? Or the better question is, did it intend to stop at ruba', or was the idea of a multiple established, so that the Qur'an did not need to proceed in multiples to infinity, khumas (five times), sudas (six times), and so on? Furthermore, the ayah did not stop with the number but continued to warn that you should not do so if you fear you cannot treat them equally, an important point since each is accountable for his actions. The verse also provides the answer to those who fear their inability to treat more than one wife equally: to take only one wife from among the orphans, presumably if they were not already married. If already married, then keep "ma malakat aymanakum" (what your right hands possess), which could mean a wife already held by a man or a captive held by the tribe. This point is controversial and would hardly be agreed upon by most Qur'anic interpreters. Yet the Qur'an uses the words *malakat* and *yamin* in different ways that could lead us to suppose that the interpretation given here is as valid as the ones that see them as indicating slaves, as explained earlier.

The most important point to emphasize here, however, is that all the possible actions set out for men by the Qur'an in S. 4:3 are based on accountability. Men will be judged according to their actions, so if they fear their inability to act with justice, that should provide them with the answers as to how to proceed. Taking more than one wife is clearly included among those actions that could lead to injustice and to harming others, and men should fear taking such a road.

Conclusions

A number of theses are presented in this chapter. First and foremost is the historical fact that interpretation of the Qur'an, and hence formulation of Islamic law, has been largely a male prerogative. Few women have ventured into Qur'anic interpretation, and those who have, have done so with caution and without becoming immersed in issues of gender and the laws pertaining to gender.

Second, because of the history of Qur'anic interpretation and the lack of women's active and formal participation, Islamic law has been and continues to be patriarchal. Interestingly, the modern period has seen an increase in this patriarchal dominance even while nation-states claim to have improved the lives and rights of women through constitutions and guarantees of equal opportunity in education and employment.

Third, it is in the realm of relations between males and females that patriarchal tightening exists and continues. While women before the modernization of law had access to divorce, and could leave marriages they felt were causing them harm, modern shari'ah laws—as interpreted through patriarchal judicial committees and almost exclusively male national assemblies—have all but denied them such a right, unless the husband is also willing to divorce. This change has come about through legal codes based literally on fiqh texts selected and interpreted by a modern patriarchal order, one that has added state power to male biological power to ensure men's control of women. In this, the state has acted as a male patriarch, extending and enforcing male power. This is in contrast to earlier conditions, before the omnipotence of the centralized nation-state, when society had greater control over its own laws and a judge judged according to the case brought to his court. His intent was to arbitrate fairly and not to enforce the codes created by state structures.

Whereas the shariʿah is normally blamed for the unequal gender relations under which Muslim women live today, this chapter shows that the shariʿah today is interpreted and applied differently from other historical periods. Which brings us to the fourth major point made here. Because scholars have used fiqh literature in all its types—exegetics, fatawa—as their sole source for studying the history of women, the normative picture is based on such sources. But these sources, including the writings of various schools of law, have to be studied in conjunction with the actual application of these laws for us to understand women's history. When legal interpretation is the product of one mind under certain conditions of time and place, this interpretation can neither be complete nor binding on all Muslims in all places, or even in the same time period. The concrete evidence of legal decisions can tell us how laws were applied and hence interpreted from one age to another. It is only by comparing the implementation of laws before and after the coming of the nation-state that we can determine the actual contribution of nation-states to gender inequality, and what is established by nation-states can be disestablished by them.

Notes

1. While it is usual to translate the term *fuqaha'* as "jurists," I find that translation somewhat inaccurate. A jurist sets the laws that are applied in courts. Fuqahaʿ only state legal opinion that is nonbinding in court. Since the fuqahaʿ are technically religious persons recognized as such by their peers and by society at large, the term "clergy" is more appropriate. In this sense any Muslim clergyman is a *faqih*, but the term is reserved for those who are particularly recognized for their learning and intellectual discourses.

2. See Dalenda Largueche, "Confined, Battered, and Repudiated Women in Tunis since the Eighteenth Century," in *Women, the Family, and Divorce Laws in Islamic History*, ed. Amira El-Azhary Sonbol (Syracuse, N.Y.: Syracuse University Press, 1996), 259–76.

3. For more about these issues, please see the various chapters in Sonbol, *Women, the Family, and Divorce Law in Islamic History*.

4. Egypt, National Archives, *Dumyat al-sharʿiyya* (1011), 43:84–182.

5. See, for example, the image of Si al-Sayyid, the oriental despot model of a husband created by Najib Mahfouz in his trilogy.

6. Suraiya Faroqhi, *Making a Living in the Ottoman Lands, 1480 to 1820* (Istanbul: Isis Press, 1995), 88, 132.

7. Afaf Lutfi al-Sayyid Marsot, *Men and Women in Eighteenth Century Egypt* (Austin: University of Texas Press, 1997).

8. Egypt, National Archives, Alexandria al-Sharʿiyya (1130), 65:306–170.

9. Particularly Shaykhs Muhammad ʿAbdu and Jamal al-Din al-Afghani.

10. Abu al-Faraj b. al-Jawzi, *Ahkam al-Nisa'* (Cairo: Maktabat al-Turath al-Islami, 1984), 4. My translation.

11. Ibid., 39–40.

12. Ibid.

13. 'Abd al-Mit'al M. Al-Jabri, *Al-Ma'rah fi'l-Tasawwur al-Islami* (Woman in Islamic Perception), 6th ed. (Cairo: Maktabat Wahba, 1983), 92–93.

14. Fazlur Rahman, *Islam: Ideology and the Way of Life* (London: Muslim Schools Trust, 1980), 396–98.

15. Rashad Khalifa, *Qur'an: The Final Scripture* (Tucson, Ariz.: Islamic Productions International, 1981); his translation.

16. The words in parentheses are my own, the word *qint* ("obedience") being of great importance. Yusuf Ali indicates that it is generally accepted as meaning obedience to a husband; in fact, it means obedience to God, submissiveness, and humbleness as characteristics of piety.

17. Ibn al-Jawzi, *Ahkam al-Nisa'*, 80.

18. Quoted in Mahmud al-Sabbagh, *Al-Sa'ada al-Zawjiyyah fi'l-Islam* (Cairo: Makabat al-Salam al-'alamiyyah, 1985), 134. My translation.

19. Hans Wehr, *Arabic-English Dictionary: The Hans Wehr Dictionary of Modern Written Arabic*, ed. J. M. Cowan (Ithaca, N.Y.: Spoken Language Services, 1976), 968.

20. Quoted in Al-Sabbagh, *Al-Sa'ada al-Zawjiyyah*, 137.

21. Rahman, *Islam*, 396.

22. *Mawsu'at al-Hadith al-Sharif*, Sahih al-Bukhari, Tafsir al-Qur'an, *Hadith* no. 4207, p. 45.

23. Ibid.

24. Sakhr, *Mawsu'at al-Hadith al-Sharif*, Sahih al-Bukhari, *Al-Nikah*-47.

25. Ibid., Muwatta' of Malik, al-Nikah-16.

26. Muhammad Shahrour, *al-Kitab wa'l-Qur'an, Qira'ah Mu'asirah* (Damascus: al-Ahali l'il-Tiba'ah wa'l-Nashr wa'l-Tawzi', 1990), 597.

27. Al-Sayyid Sabiq, *Fiqh al-Sunna* (Beirut: Dar al-Kitab al-'Arabi, 1987), 2:107–8.

28. Ibid., 2:105.

29. See Sonbol, *Women, the Family, and Divorce Laws in Islamic History*.

30. See Abdal-Rahim Abdal-Rahman Abdal-Rahim, "The Family and Gender Laws in Egypt during the Ottoman Period," ibid., 96.

Bibliography

Abugideiri, Hibba. "Allegorical Gender: The Figure of Eve Revisited." *American Journal of Islamic Social Sciences* 13, no. 4 (Winter 1996): 518–35.

Ahmad, Khurshid, and Zafar Ishaq Ansari, eds. *Islamic Perspectives: Studies in Honour of Mawlana Sayyid Abul 'Ala' Mawdudi*. London: The Islamic Foundation, 1979.

Ahmed, Leila. *Women and Gender in Islam*. New Haven: Yale University Press, 1992.

Ali, A. Yusuf, trans. *The Holy Qur'an: Text, Translation, and Commentary*. Brentwood, Md.: Amana Corp., 1983.

'Ashur, Sa'id Harun. *Fiqh Sirat Nisa' al-Nabiyy: Mawaqif wa Qadaya*. Cairo: Al-Qahira Al-Haditha lil-Tiba'a.

al-Bawwab, Sulayman Salim. *Mi'a Awa'il min al-Nisa*. Damascus: Dar al-Hikmah, 1992.

Bellis, Alice Ogden. *Helpmates, Harlots, and Heroes*. Louisville, Ky.: Westminster/John Knox Press, 1994.

Bukhari, Muhammad ibn Ismail. *Sahih al-Bukhari: The Early Years of Islam*. Gibraltar: Dar al-Andalus, 1981.

Burns, J. Patout. *Theological Anthropology*. Philadelphia: Fortress, 1981.

Carr, Anne. *Transforming Grace: Christian Tradition and Women's Experience*. San Francisco, Calif.: Harper and Row, 1988.

Ceplair, Larry. *The Public Years of Sarah and Angelina Grimké: Selected Writing, 1835–1839*. New York: Columbia University Press, 1989.

Christ, Carol. *The Laughter of Aphrodite: Reflections on a Journey to the Goddess*. San Francisco, Calif.: Harper and Row, 1987.

Cole, W. G. *Sex in Christianity and Psychoanalysis*. London: Dent, 1956.

The Concise History of Women's Suffrage: Selections from the Classic Work of Stanton, Anthony, Gage, and Harper. Bloomington: Indiana University Press, 1978.

Crone, Patricia, and Mark Cohen. *Hagarism: The Making of the Islamic World*. Cambridge: Cambridge University Press, 1977.

Daly, Mary. *The Church and the Second Sex*. New York: Harper and Row, 1968.

———. *Beyond God the Father: Toward a Philosophy of Women's Liberation*. Boston: Beacon Press, 1973.

———. *The Church and the Second Sex*. 2d ed. Boston: Beacon Press, 1985.

Egypt. National Archives. Shari'a court records for Alexandria and Dumyat.

Fabella, Virginia, and Sun Ai Lee Park. *We Dare to Dream: Doing Theology on Asian Women*. Maryknoll, N.Y.: Orbis Books, 1989.

Faroqhi, Suraiya. *Making a Living in the Ottoman Lands, 1480 to 1820*. Istanbul: The Isis Press, 1995.

Fernea, Elizabeth Warnock. "Foreword." In *Women, the Family and Divorce Laws in Islamic History*, ed. Amira El-Azhary Sonbol, ix–xi. New York: Syracuse University Press, 1996.

———. *In Search of Islamic Feminism*. New York: Doubleday, 1998.

Finson, Shelley Davis. *Women and Religion: A Bibliographic Guide to Christian Feminist Liberation Theology*. Toronto: University of Toronto Press, 1991.

Fiorenza, Elisabeth Schuessler. *In Memory of Her: A Feminist Theological Reconstruction of Christian Origins*. New York: Crossroad, 1983.

———. *Jesus in Bread, Not Stone*. Boston: Beacon Press, 1984.

———. *But She Said*. Boston: Beacon Press, 1992.

———. *Discipleship of Equals: A Critical Feminist Ekklesialogy of Liberation*. New York: Crossroad, 1993.

———. *Jesus, Miriam's Child, Sophia's Prophet: Critical Issues in Feminist Christology*. New York: Continuum, 1994.

———, ed. *Searching the Scriptures: A Feminist Commentary*. 2 vols. New York: Crossroad, 1994.

Friedan, Betty. *The Feminine Mystique*. New York: Norton, 1963; Dell Publishing Company, 1983.

El-Geyoushi, Muhammad Ibraheem. *The Meaning of Islam*. Cairo: Wahba Book Shop.

al-Husayni, Mubashshir al-Tarazi. *Al-Mar'ah wa Huquqiha fi'l-Islam*. Cairo: n.p., 1977.

Ibn Ishaq, Muhammad. *Mukhtasar Sirat Ibn Hisham: Al-Sirah al-Nabawiyah*. Beirut: Dar al-Nafais, 1977.

Ibn al-Jawzi, Abu'l Faraj. *Ahkam al-Nisa'*. Cairo: Maktabat al-Turath al-Islami, 1984.

Ibn Kathir, Isma'il ibn Umar. *Al-Bidayah wa'al-Nihayah*. Cairo: Matba'at al-Sa'adah, 1939.

———. *Tafsir Ibn Kathir*. Cairo: Dar al-Hadith, 1990.

al-Jabri, 'Abd al-Mit'al Muhammad. *Al-Mar'ah fi'l-Tasawwur al-Islami*. 6th ed. Cairo: Maktabat Wahba, 1983.

Johnson, Elizabeth. *She Who Is: The Mystery of God in Feminist Theological Discourse*. New York: Crossroad, 1992.

Kakhia, Tariq Isma'il. *Al-Zawaj al-Islami*. 2d ed. Hims, Syria: Mu'assasat al-Zu'bi lil-Tiba'ah wa'l-Nashr.

Khung, Chung Hyun. "Han Pu-ri: Doing Theology from Korean Women's Perspective." In *We Dare to Dream: Doing Theology on Asian Women,* ed. Virginia Fabella and Sun Ai Lee Park. Maryknoll, N.Y.: Orbis Books, 1989.

———. *The Struggle to Be the Sun Again: Introducing Asian Women's Theology.* Maryknoll, N.Y.: Orbis Books, 1989.

Kuhn, Thomas. *The Structure of Scientific Revolutions.* 2d ed. Chicago: University of Chicago Press, 1970.

Kvam, Kristen E., Linda S. Schearing, and Valerie H. Ziegler, eds. *Eve and Adam: Jewish, Christian, and Muslim Readings on Genesis and Gender.* Bloomington: Indiana University Press, 1999.

LaCugna, Catherine M., ed. *Freeing Theology: The Essentials of Theology in Feminist Perspective.* San Francisco, Calif.: Harper, 1993.

Laffey, Alice. *Appreciating God's Creation Through Scripture.* New York: Paulist Press, 1997.

———. *An Introduction to the Old Testament: A Feminist Perspective.* Philadelphia: Fortress Press, 1988.

———. "Tanakh, Bible, and Qur'an: Assumptions and Methods of Interpretation." In *Religions of the Book: The 1992 Annual Publication of the College Theology Society,* ed. Gerard Sloyan, 38:49–64. Washington, D.C.: The University of America Press, 1996.

Largueche, Dalenda. "Confined, Battered, and Repudiated Women in Tunis since the Eighteenth Century." In *Women, the Family and Divorce Laws in Islamic History,* ed. Amira Sonbol, 259–76. Syracuse, N.Y.: Syracuse University Press, 1996.

Levine, Suzanne, and Harriet Lyons, eds. *The Decade of Women: A Ms. History of the Seventies in Words and Pictures.* New York: Putnam, 1980.

Lienesch, Michael. *Redeeming America: Piety and Politics in the New Christian Right.* Chapel Hill: University of North Carolina Press, 1993.

Lutfi al-Sayyid Marsot, Afaf. *Men and Women in Eighteenth Century Egypt.* Austin: University of Texas Press, 1997.

Mazrui, Ali A. "Islam in a More Conservative Western World." *American Journal of Islamic Social Sciences* 13, no. 2 (Summer 1996):246–49.

Mbiti, John. *African Religions and Philosophy.* Garden City, N.Y.: Doubleday, 1970.

al-Midani, Shaykh Muhammad M. *Al-Mujtamaʿ al-Islami Kama Tunazzimahu Surat al-Nisaʾ.* Cairo: Al-Majlis al-Aʿla liʾl-Shuʾun al-Islamiyya, 1973.

Nautin, Pierre, ed. *Origen, Homelies sur Jeremie.* Sources Chrétiennes 232. Paris: Cerf, 1976.

Newsom, Carol, and Nancy Ringe, eds. *The Women's Bible Commentary.* Louisville, Ky.: Westminster/John Knox Press, 1992.

Oduyoye, Mercy Amba. "Reflections from a Third World Woman's Perspective." In *The Irruption of the Third World: Challenge to Theology,* ed. Virginia Fabella and Sergio Torres, 246–55. Maryknoll, N.Y.: Orbis Books, 1983.

———. *Daughters of Anowa: African Women and Patriarchy.* Maryknoll, N.Y.: Orbis Books, 1995.

Oduyoye, Mercy Amba, and Virginia Fabella, eds. *With Passion and Compassion: Third World Women Doing Theology.* Maryknoll, N.Y.: Orbis Books, 1988.

Okure, Theresa. "Commentary on the Gospel of John." In *The New International Bible Commentary.* Liturgical Press, 1998.

Pieris, Aloysius. *An Asian Theology of Liberation.* Maryknoll, N.Y.: Orbis Books, 1988.

Rahman, Fazlur. *Islam: Ideology and the Way of Life.* London: Muslim Schools Trust, 1980.

al-Razi, Fakhr al-Din Muhammad ibn Umar. *Al-Tafsir al-Kabir.* Cairo: n.p., 1934–62.

Ruether, Rosemary Radford. *New Women, New Earth: Sexist Ideologies and Human Liberation.* New York: Seabury Press, 1975.

———. *Sexism and God-talk: Toward a Feminist Theology.* Boston: Beacon Press, 1983, 1993.

———. *Women Church: Theology and Practice.* San Francisco: Harper and Row, 1988.

———. *Gaia and God.* San Francisco: Harper, 1992.

———. "Christianity and Women in the Modern World." In *Today's Women in World Religion,* ed. Arvind Sharma, 267–302. Albany: SUNY Press, 1994.

———, ed. *Religion and Sexism: Images of Women in the Jewish and Christian Traditions.* New York: Simon and Schuster, 1974.

Ruether, Rosemary Radford, and Eleanor McLaughlin, eds. *Women of Spirit: Female Leadership in the Jewish and Christian Traditions.* New York: Simon and Schuster, 1979.

Ruether, Rosemary Radford, Marc Ellis, and Naim Ateek, eds. *Faith and the Intifada: Palestinian Christian Voices.* Boston: Beacon, 1992.

al-Sabbagh, Mahmud. *Al-Sa'adah al-Zawjiyyah fi'l-Islam.* Cairo: Maktabat al-Salam al-'Alamiyyah, 1985.

Sabiq, al-Sayyid. *Fiqh al-Sunna.* Vol. 2. Beirut: Dar al-Kitab al-'Arabi, 1987.

Shahrour, Muhammad. *Al-Kitab wa'l-Qur'an, Qira'ah Mu'asirah.* Damascus: Al-Ahali l'il-Tiba'ah wa'l-Nashr wa'l-Tawzi', 1990.

al-Shayyal, Jaber. *Qisas al-Nisa' fi'l-Quran al-Karim.* Cairo: Maktabat al-Turath al-Islami, 1983.

Smith, Jane I. "Joining the Debate." *The World and I,* September 1, 1997.

Sonbol, Amira El-Azhary. "Law and Gender Violence in Ottoman and Modern Egypt." In *Women, the Family and Divorce Laws in Islamic History,* ed. Amira El-Azhary Sonbol. Syracuse, N.Y.: Syracuse University Press, 1996.

———. "Ta'a and Modern Legal Reform: A Rereading." *Islam and Christian-Muslim Relations* 9, no. 3 (1998):285–94.

———, ed. *Women, the Family, and Divorce Law in Islamic History.* Syracuse, N.Y.: Syracuse University Press, 1996.

Stanton, Elizabeth Cady. *The Women's Bible, 1895–1898.* Seattle: Coalition Task Force on Women and Religion, 1974.

Stowasser, Barbara Freyer. *Women in the Qur'an: Traditions and Interpretation.* New York: Oxford University Press, 1994.

———. "Gender Issues and Contemporary Quran Interpretation." In *Islam, Gender and Social Change*, ed. Yvonne Yazbeck Haddad and John L. Esposito, 30–44. New York: Oxford University Press, 1998.

Swidler, Leonard, and Arlene Swidler, eds. *Women Priests: A Catholic Commentary on the Vatican Declaration*. New York: Paulist Press, 1977.

Al-Tabari. *Tafsir al-Tabari*. Damascus: Dar al-Qalam, 1997.

Trible, Phyllis. *God and the Rhetoric of Sexuality*. Philadelphia: Fortress, 1978.

———. *Texts of Terror: Literary-Feminist Readings of Biblical Narratives*. Philadelphia: Fortress, 1984.

Wadud, Amina. *Qur'an and Woman: Rereading the Sacred Text from a Woman's Perspective*. New York: Oxford University Press, 1999.

Weems, Renita. *Just a Sister Away: A Womanist Vision of Women's Relationships in the Bible*. San Diego: LuraMedia, 1988.

Zikmund, Barbara Brown. "The Struggle for the Right to Preach." In *Women and Religion in America: The Nineteenth Century*, ed. Rosemary R. Ruether and Rosemary S. Keller, 193–240. San Francisco: Harper and Row, 1981.

———. "Women and Ordination." In *In Our Own Voices: Four Centuries of American Women's Religious Writing*, ed. Rosemary Radford Ruether and Rosemary Skinner Keller, 293–310. San Francisco: Harper, 1995.

Contributors

Hibba Abugideiri is a Ph.D. candidate in the History Department at Georgetown University. Her research has focused on the relationship between nineteenth-century Egyptian colonial medicine and gender relations. She has received fellowships from the American Research Center in Egypt and Fulbright and has published several works on women's issues within Islam.

Karen Armstrong is a freelance writer and broadcaster living in London and a former professor of modern literature at London University. Her publications include *A History of God; The 4000 Year Quest in Judaism, Christianity, and Islam; Jerusalem: One City, Three Faiths; In the Beginning: A New Interpretation of Genesis; Muhammad: A Biography of the Poet; Through the Narrow Gate;* and *The Battle for God.*

Leila Gal Berner received her Ph.D. in medieval Jewish history at UCLA and was ordained at the Reconstructionist Rabbinical College. Presently serving as a congregational rabbi, she has taught at Reed, Swarthmore, and Bryn Mawr colleges and in the Department of Religion at Emory University. She is a part-time faculty member at American University in Washington, D.C., where she teaches in the area of Jewish-Christian relations.

John L. Esposito is professor of religion and international affairs, Georgetown University, and director of the Center for Muslim-Christian Understanding at Georgetown University's Edmund A. Walsh School of Foreign Service. He is editor-in-chief of the *Oxford Encyclopedia of the*

Modern Islamic World and of the *Oxford History of Islam*. Among his publications are *The Islamic Threat: Myth or Reality?*; *Islam and Democracy*
(with John Voll); *Islam: The Straight Path; Islam and Politics; The Contemporary Islamic Revival* (with Yvonne Yazbeck Haddad and John O. Voll);
Voices of Resurgent Islam; Islam in Asia: Religion, Politics and Society; and
Women in Muslim Family Law.

Yvonne Yazbeck Haddad is professor of history of Islam and Christian-
Muslim relations at the Edmund A. Walsh School of Foreign Service at
Georgetown University. She is past president of the Middle East Studies
Association and a former editor of *Muslim World*. Her published works
include *Contemporary Islam and the Challenge of History; Islam, Gender and
Social Change* (with John Esposito); *Islamic Values in the United States* (with
Adair Lummis); *The Contemporary Islamic Revival* (with John Esposito
and John Voll); *The Islamic Understanding of Death and Resurrection* (with
Jane Smith); *The Muslims of America; Christian-Muslim Encounters* (with
Wadi Haddad); *Mission to America* (with Jane Smith); *Muslim Communities in North America* (with Jane Smith); and *Muslims on the Americaniza-
tion Path?* (with John Esposito).

Alice L. Laffey is associate professor of Old Testament at College of the
Holy Cross in Worcester, Massachusetts. Among her publications are
*The Pentateuch: A Liberation-Critical Reading; Appreciating God's Creation
through Scripture; An Introduction to the Old Testament: A Feminist Perspec-
tive; First Kings, Second Kings: Collegeville Bible Commentary 19;* and *First
Chronicles, Second Chronicles: Collegeville Bible Commentary 10.*

Amy-Jill Levine is E. Rhodes and Leona B. Carpenter professor of New
Testament studies and director of the Carpenter Program in religion,
gender, and sexuality at Vanderbilt University Divinity School. Prior to
coming to Vanderbilt, she was the Sara Lawrence Lightfoot associate
professor of religion at Swarthmore College. Holding a Ph.D. in religion
from Duke University, Levine has been awarded grants from the Mellon
Foundation, the National Endowment for the Humanities, and the American Council of Learned Societies. Her numerous books and articles address such topics as Christian origins, formative Judaism, the "Historical Jesus," and feminist scriptural interpretation.

Rosemary Radford Ruether is the Georgia Harkness professor of applied theology at Garrett Evangelical Theological Seminary and North-

western University. She is the author of thirty-five books on feminist theology, ecology, peace, and justice in Christian theological history.

Amira al-Azhari Sonbol is associate professor of Islamic history, law, and society at the Center for Muslim-Christian Understanding, Edmund A. Walsh School of Foreign Service, Georgetown University. She has published essays on Egypt and on women and Islam. Her publications include *The Creation of a Medical Profession in Egypt, 1800–1922; Women, the Family, and Divorce Law in Islamic History;* and *The New Mamluks.*

Index